Easy Beading

Vol. 8

Fast. Fashionable. Fun.

The best projects from the eighth year of *Bead Style* magazine

KALMBACH BOOKS

Kalmbach Books
21027 Crossroads Circle
Waukesha, Wisconsin 53186
www.Kalmbach.com/books

Published in 2012

15 14 13 12 11   1 2 3 4 5

Printed in China

ISBN: 978-0-87116-481-0

The material in this book has appeared previously in *Bead Style* magazine. *Bead Style* is registered as a trademark.

Editor: Erica Swanson
Proofreader: Karin Van Vorhees
Art Director: Lisa Bergman
Page Layout: Rebecca Markstein

Publisher's Cataloging-In-Publication Data

Easy beading. Vol. 8 : fast, fashionable, fun : the best projects from the
  eighth year of Bead Style magazine.

    p. : ill. (chiefly col.) ; cm.

  "The material in this book has appeared previously in Bead Style magazine."--copyright page.
    Includes index.
    ISBN: 978-0-87116-481-0

  1. Beadwork--Handbooks, manuals, etc. 2. Beads--Handbooks, manuals, etc. 3. Jewelry making--Handbooks, manuals, etc. I. Title. II. Title: Bead Style Magazine.

TT860 .E27 2012
745.594/2

Contents

COVER PAGE 238

14

GEMSTONES

34

CRYSTALS

29

71

52

METAL & CHAIN

110

MIXED MEDIA

134

138

242

216

Introduction

Welcome to the eighth volume of *Easy Beading*. I'm happy to say our contributing designers have had a particularly spectacular year — the designs in this book are gorgeous.

Each project is a personal celebration of creativity. They include new materials, fresh color combinations, and, of course, new designs from some very creative people. Best of all, each project is easily mastered with our step-by-step photos and instructions.

This volume of *Easy Beading* is once again organized by materials used:

- Gemstones
- Crystals
- Metal & chain
- Glass, ceramic, & pearls
- Mixed media

I'm sure you have a favorite, but I urge you to browse each category — you never know where you'll be inspired.

We've included projects for beginners as well as more experienced beaders. There are pieces you can make in an hour or two and some you could tackle in 15 minutes. The following pages are packed with loads of creative potential, so get those post-its out to mark your must-dos.

I hope you have as much fun with these projects as we did.

Cathy

CATHY JAKICIC,
EDITOR, *Bead Style* **MAGAZINE**
editor@beadstylemag.com

214

Beader's Glossary

A visual reference to common beads and findings

crystal and glass

 Czech fire polished

 bicone

 top-drilled bicone

 cube

 oval

 drop

 briolette

 cone

round

 saucer

 top-drilled saucer (with jump ring)

flat back

 dichroic

 lampworked

 glass flowers

 leaves

 dagger

 teardrop

fringe drops

 seed beads

 triangle

bugle

gemstone shapes

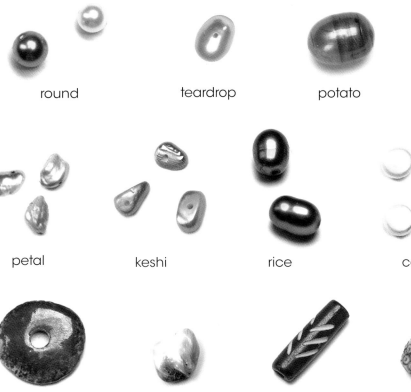

lentil   rondelle   faceted rondelle   round   oval   marquise   rectangle

tube   briolette   teardrop   chips   nugget

pearls, shells, and miscellaneous

round   teardrop   potato   button   stick

petal   keshi   rice   coin   Lucite flowers

donut   shell   bone   horn   heishi

findings, spacers, and connectors

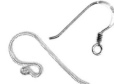
French hook
ear wires

post earring and
ear nut

hoop earring

lever-back
earring

ear
thread

magnetic
clasp

S-hook
clasp

lobster claw
clasp

toggle
clasp

two-strand
toggle clasp

box
clasp

slide
clasp

hook-and-eye
clasps

snap
clasp

pinch crimp
end

crimp
ends

coil end

crimp cone

tube bail
with loop

tube-shaped
and round crimp
beads

crimp
covers

bead tips

jump rings and
soldered jump
rings

split ring

spacers

bead
caps

pinch bail

multistrand
spacer bars

two-strand
curved tube

single-strand
tube

3-to-1 and 2-to-1
connectors

chandelier
component

bail

cone

stringing tools, materials, and chain

crimping pliers

chainnose pliers

roundnose pliers

bentnose pliers

split-ring pliers

diagonal wire cutters

heavy-duty wire cutters

ring mandrel

twisted wire beading needle

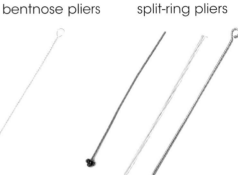

decorative head pin, head pin, eye pin

sterling silver wire

memory wire

colored craft wire

leather cord

suede cord

waxed linen

beading thread

flexible beading wire

ribbon

curb chain

rolo chain

long-and-short chain

figaro chain

fancy cable chain

11

Basics

A step-by-step reference to key jewelry-making techniques used in bead-stringing projects

plain loop

1

Trim the wire or head pin ⅜ in. (1 cm) above the top bead. Make a right-angle bend close to the bead.

2

Grab the wire's tip with round-nose pliers. The tip of the wire should be flush with the pliers. Roll the wire to form a half circle. Release the wire.

3

Reposition the pliers in the loop and continue rolling.

4

The finished loop should form a centered circle above the bead.

wrapped loop

1

Make sure you have at least 1¼ in. (3.2 cm) of wire above the bead. With the tip of your chainnose pliers, grasp the wire directly above the bead. Bend the wire (above the pliers) into a right angle.

2

Using roundnose pliers, position the jaws in the bend.

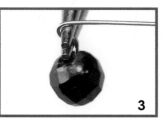

3

Bring the wire over the top jaw of the roundnose pliers.

4

Reposition the pliers' lower jaw snugly into the loop. Curve the wire downward around the roundnose pliers. This is the first half of a wrapped loop.

5

Position the chainnose pliers' jaws across the loop.

6

Wrap the wire tail around the wire stem, covering the stem between the loop and the top bead. Trim the excess wire and press the cut end close to the wraps with chainnose pliers.

opening and closing loops or jump rings

1

Hold the loop or jump ring with two pairs of chainnose pliers or chainnose and roundnose pliers, as shown.

2

To open the loop or jump ring, bring one pair of pliers toward you and push the other pair away. String materials on the open loop or jump ring. Reverse the steps to close the open loop or jump ring.

opening a split ring

Slide the hooked tip of split-ring pliers between the two overlapping wires.

overhand knot

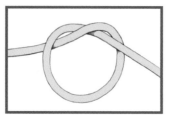

Make a loop and pass the working end through it. Pull the ends to tighten the knot.

surgeon's knot

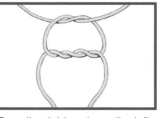

Cross the right end over the left end and go through the loop. Go through again. Pull the ends to tighten. Cross the left end over the right end and go through once. Pull the ends to tighten.

lark's head knot

Fold a cord in half and lay it behind a ring, loop, etc. with the fold pointing down. Bring the ends through the ring from back to front, then through the fold and tighten.

making wraps above a top-drilled bead

1

Center a top-drilled bead on a 3-in. (7.6 cm) piece of wire. Bend each wire upward to form a squared-off "U" shape.

2

Cross the wires into an "X" above the bead.

3

Using chainnose pliers, make a small bend in each wire to form a right angle.

4

Wrap the horizontal wire around the vertical wire as in a wrapped loop. Trim the excess wire.

folded crimp

1

Position the crimp bead in the notch closest to the crimping pliers' handle.

2

Separate the wires and firmly squeeze the crimp.

3

Move the crimp into the notch at the pliers' tip and hold the crimp as shown. Squeeze the crimp bead, folding it in half at the indentation.

4

Test that the folded crimp is secure.

flat crimp

1

Hold the crimp using the tip of your chainnose pliers. Squeeze the pliers firmly to flatten the crimp.

2

Tug the wire to make sure the crimp has a solid grip. If the wire slides, repeat the steps with a new crimp.

cutting flexible beading wire

Decide how long you want your necklace to be. Add 6 in. (15 cm) and cut a piece of beading wire to that length. (For a bracelet, add 5 in./13 cm.)

add a clasp

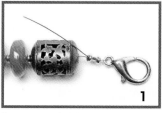

1

On one end, string a spacer, a crimp bead, a spacer, and a clasp. Go back through the last few beads strung and tighten the wire.

2

On the other end of the piece, repeat step 1, substituting a 3–4-in. (7.6–10 cm) piece of chain for the clasp if desired. Check the fit; add or remove beads if needed. On each end, crimp the crimp bead and trim the excess wire. Close a crimp cover over each crimp, if desired.

Gemstones

Create a
waterfall
necklace

Try blue amazonite to represent water and dangling pearls as the spray coming off the water.

A scene from nature inspires elegant wearable jewelry

by **Melissa Hathcock**

When I bought these beads, I had no idea
how I was going to use them — I just knew I liked them.
Then one day as I was watching a Discovery Channel
program about jungles, I was inspired by
a scenic waterfall.

1 necklace • On a 2½-in. (6.4 cm) head pin, string a faceted teardrop. Make a wrapped loop (Basics, p. 12) perpendicular to the bead. Make three teardrop units.

2 On a 1½-in. (3.8 cm) head pin, string a 7 mm pearl. Make a wrapped loop. Make 12 pearl units.

3 Cut a 2½-in. (5 cm) piece of 24-gauge wire. Make the first half of a wrapped loop on one end. String a 7 mm pearl and make a wrapped loop perpendicular to the first loop. Make four connectors.

4 Attach a pearl unit, a teardrop unit, and a pearl unit to the unwrapped loop of a connector. Complete the wraps. Make three dangles.

5 To the top loop of one dangle, attach a pearl unit, a connector, and a pearl unit. Complete the wraps.

6 Cut a piece of beading wire (Basics, p. 13). String: pearl unit, 7 mm pearl, the long dangle from step 5, 7 mm pearl, pearl unit. Center the beads on the wire.

Supplies

necklace 16 in. (41 cm)
- **3** 26 mm faceted teardrops
- 16-in. (41 cm) strand 20 mm oval gemstones
- **25** 7 mm pearls
- **12–16** 3 mm pearls
- flexible beading wire, .014 or .015
- 2 in. (5 cm) chain for extender, 4–5 mm links
- 10 in. (25 cm) 24-gauge half-hard wire
- **3** 2½-in. (6.4 cm) head pins
- **13** 1½-in. (3.8 cm) head pins
- **2** crimp beads
- S-hook clasp and soldered jump ring
- chainnose and roundnose pliers
- diagonal wire cutters
- crimping pliers (optional)

earrings
- **2** 26 mm faceted teardrops
- **6** 7 mm pearls
- 5 in. (13 cm) 24-gauge half-hard wire
- **2** 2½-in. (6.4 cm) head pins
- **3** 1½-in. (3.8 cm) head pins
- pair of earring wires
- chainnose and roundnose pliers
- diagonal wire cutters

Design alternative

Focus on the pearls for a more delicate version in a monochromatic palette.

7 On each end, string: 7 mm pearl, short dangle from step 4, 7 mm pearl, pearl unit, 7 mm pearl.

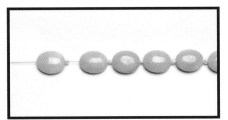

8 On each end, string an oval bead and a 3 mm pearl. Repeat until the strand is within 1 in. (2.5 cm) of the finished length.

9 Cut a 2-in. (5 cm) piece of chain for an extender. On one end, attach an S-hook clasp (Basics, p. 13). Repeat on the other end, substituting the chain for the clasp.

10 On a 1½-in. (3.8 cm) head pin, string a pearl. Make the first half of a wrapped loop. Attach the chain and complete the wraps.

Tip

You can substitute briolettes for the faceted teardrops. Turn to Basics, p. 13, to review making a set of wraps above a top-drilled bead.

"Inspiration is everywhere, if you just take the time to look."
—Melissa

1 earrings • Make a teardrop unit, two pearl units, and a connector as in necklace steps 1–3.

2 Attach the units as in step 4. Open the loop of an earring wire (Basics, p. 12) and attach the dangle. Close the loop. Make a second earring.

All in clover

Wear a springtime strand all year long

By Kelsey Lawler

I couldn't resist the fresh feel of these faceted briolettes paired with gleaming silver chain. The design is a breeze, and the effect is sweetly eye-catching.

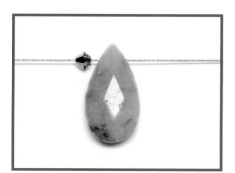

1 Cut a 10-in. (25 cm) piece of beading wire. String a bicone crystal and a briolette. Repeat the pattern eight times, then string a bicone. Center the beads.

2 Cut two 6–7-in. (15–18 cm) pieces of chain. On each end of the beaded strand, string a crimp bead, a bicone, a Wire Guardian, and an end link of a chain. Go back through the last few beads strung and tighten the wire. Crimp the crimp bead (Basics, p. 12) and trim the excess wire.

3 Check the fit and trim chain from each end if necessary. Open a jump ring (Basics, p. 12). On one end, attach the chain and a lobster claw clasp. Close the jump ring.

Supplies

necklace 17 in. (43 cm)
- **9** 22 mm briolettes
- **12** 4 mm bicone crystals
- flexible beading wire, .014 or .015
- 14–16 in. (36–41 cm) chain, 5–6 mm links
- 5 mm jump ring
- **2** crimp beads
- **2** Wire Guardians
- lobster claw clasp
- **2** pairs of pliers
- diagonal wire cutters
- crimping pliers (optional)

Supply note

These beads are pear-shaped chrysoprase, but any large briolette will work well with this design.

ADD SPARKLE
to inexpensive stones

Chips get a fresh glow when used with copper and resin

by Cathy Jakicic

Quartz, amazonite, and opal chips, plus blue agates and copper findings came together in a jewelry set with an interesting range of colors and textures.

Supplies

necklace 21 in. (53 cm)
- 50 mm swirl bezel
- 12-in. (30 cm) strand 20 mm round faceted beads
- **4** 32-in. (81 cm) strands 8–12 mm gemstone chips, in four colors
- **8** 4 mm bicone crystals
- flexible beading wire, .010 or .012
- 4 in. (10 cm) 22-gauge half-hard wire
- **8** 2-in. (5 cm) eye pins, with charms
- **2** crimp beads
- toggle clasp
- ICE Resin
- mixing cups
- plastic gloves
- safety goggles
- chainnose and roundnose pliers
- diagonal wire cutters
- hammer
- bench block or anvil
- sock or heavy plastic bag
- wooden craft sticks
- crimping pliers (optional)

bracelet
- **2** 20 mm leaf-shaped bezels
- **50–70** 8–12 mm gemstone chips

- **12** 4 mm bicone crystals
- **4** 11º seed beads
- flexible beading wire, .010 or .012
- **4** 2-in. (5 cm) eye pins, with charms
- **6** crimp beads
- toggle clasp
- ICE Resin
- mixing cups
- plastic gloves
- chainnose and roundnose pliers
- diagonal wire cutters
- hammer
- bench block or anvil
- safety goggles
- sock or heavy plastic bag
- wooden craft sticks
- crimping pliers (optional)

earrings
- **2** 22 mm swirl pendants
- **2** 8–12 mm gemstone chips
- **4** 4 mm bicone crystals
- **2** 2-in. (5 cm) eye pins, with charms
- pair of earring wires
- chainnose and roundnose pliers
- diagonal wire cutters

Patricia Healey's patinated copper bezels and findings available at Lima Beads, limabeads.com.

Design alternative

Stringing only chips, make copper the focal point with a front-clasp necklace.

4

On each side, over all four wires, string 20 mm beads until the necklace is within 1 in. (2.5 cm) of the finished length.

5

On each side, over all four wires, string a crimp bead and half of a clasp. Check the fit and add or remove beads if necessary. Go back through the beads just strung and tighten the wires. Crimp the crimp bead (Basics, p. 13) and trim the excess wire.

3

Cut four 27-in. (69 cm) pieces of beading wire. On each wire, center 7–8 in. (18–20 cm) of gemstone chips, interspersing two eye pin units. On each strand, emphasize a different chip.

Center the bead unit on the bottom chip strand and complete the wraps.

7

6

Cut a 4-in. (10 cm) piece of 22-gauge wire. With the largest part of your roundnose pliers, make a plain loop (Basics, p. 12). String a 20 mm bead and make the first half of a wrapped loop.

2

On an eye pin, string a bicone crystal and a chip. Make a wrapped loop (Basics, p. 12). Make eight eye pin units.

8

Open the bead unit's plain loop (Basics, p. 12) and attach the pendant. Close the loop.

1

necklace • Put chips in a sock or a heavy plastic bag. On a bench block or anvil, hammer enough gemstone chips to fill a swirl bezel. If you plan to make a bracelet, hammer about 50 percent more chips. Set the chip pieces in the bezel and add resin (see "Tiny treasure earrings," p. 185).

5 On each end of each wire, string a bicone and a seed bead. Allowing 1 in. (2.5 cm) for the clasp, check the fit and add or remove beads if necessary.

bracelet • Follow necklace step 1 to make two leaf-shaped bezels.

1

2 Follow necklace step 2 to make four eye pin units.

6 On each side, over both wires, string a chip, a crimp bead, and half of a clasp. Go back through the beads just strung and tighten the wires. Crimp the crimp bead and trim the excess wire.

4 On one end of each strand, string a bicone crystal, a crimp bead, and a loop of a bezel. Go back through the beads just strung and tighten the wire. Crimp the crimp bead (Basics, p. 13) and trim the excess wire.

3 Cut four 8-in. (20 cm) pieces of beading wire. On each wire, center 2–2½ in. (5–6.4 cm) of gemstone chips. Include one eye pin unit per strand.

3 Open the loop of an earring wire (Basics, p. 12). Attach the dangle and close the loop.

2 Attach the eye pin unit and the loop of a swirl charm and complete the wraps.

earrings • For each earring: On an eye pin, string a bicone crystal, a gemstone chip, and a bicone. Make the first half of a wrapped loop (Basics, p. 12).

Tips

- Before you mix the resin, fill the bezel with chips to make sure you have the amount and color mix you want.
- I used chips that matched the agate's deeper blue to make sure the bezel picked up the color of the larger stones.
- The exact one-to-one ratio of two-part resin is crucial to a successful project. The Ice Resin plunger makes it simple to get the ratio correct with even the smallest amount of resin.
- Buy four different chip strands.

"Taking a hammer to the gemstones was a bit disconcerting, but the end result is worth it." —Cathy

Supply notes

- Patricia Healey's fancy eye pins have charms already attached.
- The 4 mm bicone crystals are turquoise.

Get your wires crossed

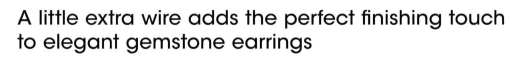

A little extra wire adds the perfect finishing touch to elegant gemstone earrings

By Ann Westby

I found these gorgeous citrine and amethyst beads at a local gem show and wanted a design that let the stones' natural beauty shine through. The subtle criss-crossed wire accent did the trick.

1 earrings • Cut a 3-in. (7.6 cm) piece of wire. String a briolette and make a set of wraps above the bead (Basics, p. 12).

2 Make the first half of a wrapped loop (Basics, p. 12).

3 Cut a 5-in. (7.6 cm) piece of wire. Make a wrapped loop. String a nugget and make a wrapped loop. Do not trim the wire.

4 Bring the wire tail across the front of the nugget and around the bottom loop. Create an X with the wire and wrap it around the stem of the top loop. Trim the excess wire.

5 Attach the briolette unit to the nugget's bottom loop with a wrapped loop and complete the wraps.

6 Open the loop of an earring wire (Basics, p. 12). Attach the wire and close the loop. Make a second earring.

Supplies

- **2** 15–20 mm nuggets
- **2** 10–13 mm briolettes
- 16 in. (41 cm) 24-gauge half-hard wire
- pair of earring wires
- chainnose and roundnose pliers
- diagonal wire cutters

23

Silver & Turquoise

A silver-banded turquoise bead is the focus of this simple bracelet

Kristal Wick

Fabric beads complement the handmade quality of the birthstone, so choose a set in a shade to highlight or contrast the blue-green tones.

Supplies

- 22 mm oval turquoise bead, with silver band
- **4** 15 mm fabric beads (Kristal Wick, kristalwick.com)
- **4** 10 mm metal saucer beads
- **4–6** 8 mm bicone crystals
- **14–16** 4 mm bicone crystals
- flexible beading wire, .014 or .015
- **2** crimp beads
- S-hook clasp and **2** soldered jump rings
- chainnose or crimping pliers
- diagonal wire cutters

1 Cut a piece of beading wire (Basics, p. 12). Center a turquoise bead on the wire.

2 On each end, string: 4 mm bicone crystal, saucer bead, 4 mm, fabric bead, 4 mm, 8 mm bicone crystal, 4 mm.

3 On each end, string: fabric bead, 4 mm, saucer, 4 mm, 8 mm, 4 mm. String alternating 8 mm and 4 mm bicones until the strand is within 1 in. (2.5 cm) of the finished length.

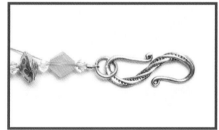

4 On each end, string a crimp bead and a soldered jump ring. Check the fit, and add or remove beads if necessary. Go back through the beads just strung and tighten the wire. Crimp the crimp bead (Basics, p. 13) and trim the excess wire. Attach an S-hook to one end.

Big beads
make for a
quick bracelet.

Weave a
chunky
chain
bracelet

Connect nuggets and chains
for an edgy bracelet

by Naomi Fujimoto

In this fun bracelet, you'll be wrapping a lot of chain, so use base metal to keep your costs in check. Try two different styles or finishes for extra pop. Also, if you're working from a spool, don't cut the chain first. Just weave a long piece and trim when you finish the bracelet.

1 bracelet • Cut a 13–16-in. (33–41 cm) piece of beading wire. String a crimp bead, a round spacer, the 12 mm (large) and 5–6 mm (small) chains, and a lobster claw clasp. Go back through the beads just strung and tighten the wire. Crimp the crimp bead (Basics, p. 12).

2 Weave the small chain through every other link of the large chain.

3 On the wire, string a nugget, a spacer, and a link of both chains.

4 About 1 in. (2.5 cm) from the links just strung, string a link of both chains.

5 On the wire, string a spacer, a crimp bead, a spacer, and two links. Go back through the beads just strung and tighten the wire. Crimp the crimp bead.

6 Trim the excess small chain. Leave a few links of large chain for an extender and trim the excess.

7 On a head pin, string a bead. Make the first half of a wrapped loop (Basics, p. 12). Attach the end link and complete the wraps.

1 earrings · Cut a five-link piece of 12 mm (large) chain. Cut a 2-in. (5 cm) piece of 5–6 mm (small) chain. Open a jump ring (Basics, p. 12). Attach an end link of each chain and the loop of an earring wire. Close the jump ring.

2 Weave the small chain through every other link of the large chain.

Design alternative

Use delicate chain to embellish seashells for earrings. To secure the wrapped chain, glue it to a few places in the back.

3 On a head pin, string a bead. Make the first half of a wrapped loop (Basics, p. 12). Attach both end links and complete the wraps. Make a second earring.

Supplies

bracelet
- 7-in. (18 cm) strand 25–40 mm nuggets
- 7–10 mm bead
- **6-8** 3–4 mm round spacers
- flexible beading wire, .018 or .019
- 14–17 in. (36–43 cm) chain, 12 mm links
- 16–19 in. (41–48 cm) chain, 5–6 mm links
- 1½-in. (3.8 cm) head pin
- **2** crimp beads
- lobster claw clasp
- chainnose and roundnose pliers
- diagonal wire cutters
- heavy-duty wire cutters (optional)

earrings
- **2** 7–10 mm beads
- **2** 1½-in. (3.8 cm) head pins
- 5 in. (13 cm) chain, 12 mm links
- 4 in. (10 cm) chain, 5–6 mm links
- **2** 5–6 mm jump rings
- pair of earring wires
- chainnose and roundnose pliers
- diagonal wire cutters
- heavy-duty wire cutters (optional)

Simple
seaside
strand

**String jasper in shades
of sand and surf**

by Joan Williams

Aqua terra jasper
was used for this
necklace, but
any gemstone in
shades of blue and
brown will work.

Although I've been a Midwesterner all my life, I absolutely adore the ocean — so much so that it inspired this necklace. As soon as I spotted this strand of aqua terra jasper, I knew exactly how it should look. The unique cut and color of the beads capture the beauty of teal-blue seas and sandy shores with little help from me.

1 Cut a piece of beading wire (Basics, p. 12). String 9–10 in. (23–25 cm) of stick beads. Center the beads.

2 On each end, string: spacer, round bead, spacer, round, spacer, faceted rondelle. Repeat until the strand is within 1 in. (2.5 cm) of the finished length.

3 On each end, string a crimp bead, a ¼-in. (6 mm) piece of French (bullion) wire, and half of a toggle clasp. Check the fit, and add or remove beads if necessary. Add a clasp (Basics, p. 13) and trim the excess wire.

Supplies

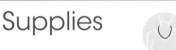

necklace 20 in. (51 cm)
- 16-in. (41 cm) strand 10–24 mm stick beads, top drilled
- **8–16** 8 mm round beads
- **4–8** 4 mm faceted rondelles
- **14–26** 2 mm spacers
- flexible beading wire, .014 or .015
- **2** crimp beads
- ½ in. (1.3 cm) French (bullion) wire
- toggle clasp
- chainnose or crimping pliers
- diagonal wire cutters

Tip

Joan attaches a clasp with both security and aesthetics in mind: "I like to use tornado crimps and French (bullion) wire on all of my pieces for a more finished look."

❝If creating makes you happy, always make time for it, no matter how busy you are.❞ —Joan

Design alternative

Any top-drilled sticks will work with this design, so play with textures and colors. A rainbow of smooth, dyed gemstones is a bright twist on the earthy feel of the original piece.

START at the FINISH

An eye-catching clasp sets the tone

by Wenche Brennbakk

When I stumble upon a must-have component, I snatch it up whether or not I have a design in mind. That's the story behind this vintage jade box clasp — it sat in my workroom for ages, waiting for the right beads to come along.

These briolettes are green fluorite.

Mother-of-pearl teardrops are a budget-friendly option.

1 On a head pin, string a flat spacer and a crystal. Make a wrapped loop (Basics, p. 12). Make 12–16 crystal units and 12–16 round-bead units.

2 Cut a piece of beading wire (Basics, p. 13). Center an accent bead on the wire.

Supplies

- ◆ 12–14 mm focal bead
- ◆ **18–24** 13–15 mm teardrop beads, top drilled
- ◆ **4** 7–9 mm briolettes
- ◆ **12–16** 6–7 mm crystals
- ◆ **12–16** 3–4 mm round beads
- ◆ **12–16** 3–4 mm flat spacers
- ◆ **10–14** 2–3 mm spacers
- ◆ flexible beading wire, .014 or .015
- ◆ **24–32** 1½-in. (3.8 cm) head pins
- ◆ **2** crimp beads
- ◆ **2** crimp covers
- ◆ 20–30 mm box clasp
- ◆ chainnose and roundnose pliers
- ◆ diagonal wire cutters
- ◆ crimping pliers (optional)

3 On each end, string a crystal unit, two round-bead units, a crystal unit, and three 13–15 mm teardrop beads.

4 On each end, string a 2–3 mm spacer and two 7–9 mm briolettes.

5 On each end, string: 2–3 mm spacer, three teardrops, 2–3 mm spacer, crystal unit, two round units, crystal unit. Repeat until the strand is within 1 in. (2.5 cm) of the finished length.

6 On each end, add a clasp (Basics, p. 13).

7 Use chainnose or crimping pliers to close a crimp cover over each crimp.

66 Norway is my home, but it's been my dream to be published in a foreign beading magazine. Now it's actually happening, and that is so cool! 99 –Wenche

Spring
breeze
bracelet

Mix shades of green
in a simple bracelet

by Debbie Tuttle

These briolettes flip back and forth with just a hint of sparkle. When you make your bracelet, be sure to fully close the plain loops, and use heavier flexible beading wire so the bead units don't fall off. You can also try glass briolettes.

1 On a head pin, string a crystal. Make a plain loop (Basics, p. 12). Make 12–14 crystal units.

2 Cut a 3-in. (7.6 cm) piece of 24-gauge wire. String a briolette and make a set of wraps above it (Basics, p. 12). Make a wrapped loop (Basics, p. 12).

3 Cut a piece of beading wire (Basics, p. 13). String two briolettes and a crystal unit. Repeat until the strand is within 1 in. (2.5 cm) of the finished length.

4 On each end, add a clasp, using a Wire Guardian if desired (Basics, p. 13).

5 Open a jump ring (Basics, p. 12). Attach the briolette unit, a crystal unit, and the loop half of the clasp. Close the jump ring.

Supplies

- **25–29** 12–14 mm briolettes
- **12–14** 8 mm round crystals
- **2** 4 mm large-hole spacers
- flexible beading wire, .018 or .019
- 3 in. (7.6 cm) 24-gauge wire
- **12–14** 1½-in. (3.8 cm) head pins
- 5–6 mm jump ring
- **2** crimp beads
- **2** Wire Guardians (optional)
- toggle clasp
- chainnose and roundnose pliers
- diagonal wire cutters
- crimping pliers (optional)

Crystals

CRYSTALLIZE
a tourmaline theme

Emulate the look of gemstones with bicones

by Leah Hanoud

The color gradations in watermelon tourmaline inspired this crystal creation: I combined crystals in shades of olive, red, and pink in a simple pattern. Though the design is bold, the colors are subtle and muted. Find your own inspiration and blend beautiful colors!

1 earrings • On a head pin, string a 5 mm, a 4 mm, and a 3 mm bicone crystal. Using the largest part of your roundnose pliers, make the first half of a wrapped loop (Basics, p. 12).

2 Attach the bead unit and a diamond-shaped link. Complete the wraps.

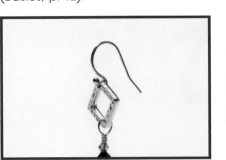

3 Open the loop of an earring wire (Basics, p. 12). Attach the dangle and close the loop. Make a second earring.

❝The simplest of techniques can produce extraordinary pieces when the colors are right.❞ —Leah

36

Tip

When finishing the necklace, make sure to include the spacer in step 3 (p. 38). It serves as a stopper so the crystals don't get pulled against the cones.

This necklace is easier than it looks: String the same pattern on each strand.

2 Attach cones, a clasp, and a chain extender (Finishing with cones, p. 38).

1 necklace • Cut nine pieces of beading wire (Basics, p. 13). On each wire, center three garnet bicone crystals. On each end of each wire, string the following bicone crystals: seven burgundy, seven rose satin, 10 olivine AB, four garnet, eight burgundy, 10 rose satin, six to 10 olivine AB.

Finishing with cones

1 Cut a 4-in. (10 cm) piece of 22-gauge wire and make a wrapped loop (Basics, p. 12). Repeat.

2 On each side, separate the strands into three sets of three wires. For each set, over all three wires, string a crimp bead and the wrapped loop. Check the fit; add or remove beads if necessary. For each set of wires, go back through the crimp bead and a few adjacent beads. Tighten the wires and crimp the crimp beads (Basics, p. 13).

3 On each end, string a spacer, a cone, and an olivine AB bicone crystal. Make the first half of a wrapped loop.

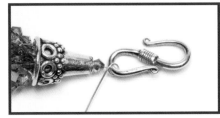

4 On one end, attach the loop and an S-hook clasp. Complete the wraps. Repeat on the other end, substituting a 2-in. (5 cm) piece of chain for the clasp.

5 On a decorative head pin, string a bicone. Make the first half of a wrapped loop. Make four bicone units in different colors.

6 Attach each unit to the end links of the chain extender. Complete the wraps as you go.

Design alternative

If you like the look of tourmaline but not its price, try a strand of ruby zoisite. You'll find similar shades of green, black, and pink at a fraction of the cost.

Supplies

earrings
- **2** 5 mm bicone crystals
- **2** 4 mm bicone crystals
- **2** 3 mm bicone crystals
- **2** 10–12 mm diamond-shaped links
- **2** 1½-in. (3.8 cm) head pins
- pair of earring wires
- chainnose and roundnose pliers
- diagonal wire cutters

necklace 18 in. (46 cm)
- 4 mm bicone crystals
  291–363 olivine AB
  307 rose satin
  271 burgundy
  100 garnet
- **2** 4 mm round or saucer spacers
- flexible beading wire, .014 or .015
- 8 in. (20 cm) 22-gauge half-hard wire
- **4** 1½-in. (3.8 cm) decorative head pins
- **2** cones
- **6** crimp beads
- S-hook clasp
- 2 in. (5 cm) chain for extender, 5–6 mm links
- chainnose and roundnose pliers
- diagonal wire cutters
- crimping pliers (optional)

Diamond drops

Bend 20-gauge wire into triangles to highlight shapely crystals

By Karen Karon

A few tools and four quick steps is all it takes to make these simple earrings.

1 Cut a 4-in. (10 cm) piece of wire. Make a plain loop (Basics, p. 12). Trim the loop to make a C-shaped hook.

2 String: spacer, rondelle, crystal, rondelle, spacer. Holding the C facing away from you, make a 45-degree bend.

Supplies

- ◆ **2** 10–14 mm crystals
- ◆ **4** 5–7 mm crystal rondelles
- ◆ **4** 3–4 mm spacers
- ◆ **8** in. (20 cm) 20-gauge half-hard wire
- ◆ roundnose pliers
- ◆ diagonal wire cutters
- ◆ metal file or emery board

3 Place your roundnose pliers 1¼ in. (3.2 cm) from the first bend. Pull the wire down to form a triangle.

4 Hook the wire in the C. Use the tip of your pliers to make a slight bend. Trim the wire and file the ends. Make a second earring.

Wrap an elegant bracelet & earrings

When the bracelet is worn with the reflective side up, the beads appear to float on your wrist.

Beading wire: They don't call it flexible for nothing

by Diane Whiting

Sometimes it's a challenge to juggle all of my projects, but this bracelet was quick and easy from start to finish. I took advantage of flexible beading wire because it's pliable (you can wrap it around beads without kinking it) and adaptable (it's a pretty design element). Satin gold or satin silver wire looks luxurious when wrapped around twist crystals.

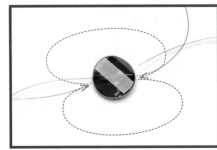

1 bracelet • Cut a 72-in. (1.8 m) piece of beading wire. Center a 22 mm twist crystal on the wire. String each end of the wire through the crystal in opposite directions. String both ends through again, so you have four strands showing on top of the crystal.

18 mm

2 On one end, string an 18 mm twist crystal. Wrap the wire around and through the crystal four times. Repeat on the other end.

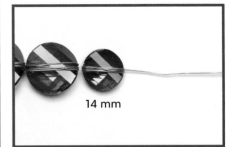

14 mm

3 On one end, string a 14 mm twist crystal. Wrap the wire around and through the crystal four times. Repeat on the other end. String two more 14 mms on each end, wrapping the wire around and through each crystal four times.

> **"I** live in a very small, old house, so I bead in my living room. My couch is my workspace." —Diane

Supplies

bracelet
- ◆ 22 mm twist crystal
- ◆ **2** 18 mm twist crystals
- ◆ **6–8** 14 mm twist crystals
- ◆ flexible beading wire, .015, in satin gold
- ◆ **2** crimp beads
- ◆ **2** crimp covers
- ◆ **2** Wire Guardians
- ◆ magnetic clasp (Star's Clasps, starsclasps.com).
- ◆ crimping pliers
- ◆ diagonal wire cutters

earrings
- ◆ **2** 18 mm twist crystals
- ◆ **2** 14 mm twist crystals
- ◆ flexible beading wire, .015, in satin gold
- ◆ **2** crimp beads
- ◆ **2** crimp covers
- ◆ pair of lever-back earring wires
- ◆ crimping pliers
- ◆ diagonal wire cutters

1 earrings • Cut a 20-in. (51 cm) piece of beading wire. Center an 18 mm twist crystal on the wire. With one end, go around and through the crystal twice.

2 With the other end, go around and through the crystal once, then over the front of the crystal, anchoring the wire under a previous wrap.

3 Over both ends, string a 14 mm twist crystal. With both ends, go around and through the crystal twice.

4 Over both ends, string a crimp bead and the loop of an earring wire. Go back through the crimp bead and tighten the wire. Crimp the crimp bead (Basics, p. 13) and trim the excess wire. Close a crimp cover over the crimp. Make a second earring.

4 On each end, add a Wire Guardian and a clasp (Basics, p. 13). Close a crimp cover over each crimp.

Design alternative

I substituted crystals in silver shade and satin silver beading wire.

Make a sparkling necklace and earrings that celebrate nature's beauty

by Suzanne Walters

Include both clear and opaque crystals to add depth to this jewelry set.

CRYSTAL
sand & surf

Before moving to Colorado, I spent my life in Huntington Beach, Calif. The pale blue water and golden sand inspired this necklace and earrings. The jewelry is simple and light, yet the detail — wrapping all of the crystals — makes it special. If you opt for a set in different colors, start by selecting the polygon pendants, since they are available in fewer colors than the bicones.

Supplies

necklace 19 in. (48 cm)
- **2** 17 mm crystal polygon pendants, in two colors
- **43–49** 6 mm bicone crystals
- **86–98** 4 mm bicone crystals, in two colors
- **22–26 in.** (56–66 cm) long-and-short chain, 7 mm links
- **129–147** 1½-in. (3.8 cm) head pins
- **4** 5 mm jump rings
- lobster claw clasp
- chainnose and roundnose pliers
- diagonal wire cutters

earrings
- **2** 17 mm crystal polygon pendants
- **4** 6 mm bicone crystals, in two colors
- **6** 4 mm bicone crystals, in three colors
- 1 in. (2.5 cm) long-and-short chain, 7 mm links
- **10** 1½-in. (3.8 cm) head pins
- **2** 5 mm jump rings
- pair of earring wires
- chainnose and roundnose pliers
- diagonal wire cutters

1 necklace • On a head pin, string a 4 mm bicone crystal. Make the first half of a wrapped loop (Basics, p. 12). Make 86 to 98 4 mm bicone units in two colors, and 43 to 49 6 mm bicone units. Set aside two 4 mm units and a 6 mm unit for step 7.

2 Cut a 1-in. (2.5 cm) piece of chain with short links on each end. Open a jump ring (Basics, p. 12). Attach an end link and a polygon pendant. Close the jump ring. Attach two sets of 4 mm and 6 mm units to the chain's two short links in the center of the chain. On the other end, attach a 4 mm unit. Attach a second 4 mm unit to the loop of the first. Attach a 6 mm unit to the second 4 mm unit. Complete the wraps as you go.

3 Cut a ½-in. (1.3 cm) piece of chain with short links on each end. Use a jump ring to attach an end link and a polygon pendant. Attach two 4 mm units and a 6 mm unit to a short link on the other end as in step 2.

4 Cut a 9–10-in. (23–25 cm) piece of chain and a second piece 1½ in. (3.8 cm) longer. Each piece should have three short links on each end. On a short link on each chain, attach two 4 mm units and a 6 mm unit as in step 2. Repeat, attaching bicone units to short links at equal intervals, until you've covered the desired length of chain.

5 Use a jump ring to attach a beaded chain, the pendant dangles, and the second beaded chain.

6 Check the fit and trim chain if necessary. Use a jump ring to attach a lobster claw clasp and the end link of the 9–10-in. (23–25 cm) beaded chain.

7 On the end link of the other beaded chain, attach two 4 mm units and one 6 mm unit as in step 2.

1 earrings • For each earring: On a head pin, string a 4 mm bicone crystal. Make the first half of a wrapped loop (Basics, p. 12). Make three 4 mm units and two 6 mm units. Complete the wraps on one 4 mm unit.

Attach the loops of the two remaining 4 mm units and complete the wraps. Attach a 6 mm unit to the loop of a 4 mm unit. Complete the wraps.

2 Cut a piece of chain with one long link and two short links. Open a jump ring (Basics, p. 12). Attach a polygon pendant and the end short link. Close the jump ring.

3 Open the loop of an earring wire (Basics, p. 12). Attach a 4 mm unit, a loop of the connected unit, and the dangle. Close the loop.

Amethyst hoops

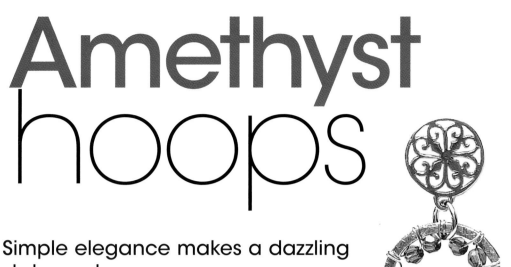

Simple elegance makes a dazzling statement

By Jenny Van

You may have seen earrings like these in stores and catalogs, but who'd guess they'd be so easy to make? Celebrate your love for purple with these lovely earrings.

1 Cut a 12-in. (30 cm) piece of wire. Secure the end by wrapping it tightly three times around a 20 mm ring.

2 String a crystal. Holding the bead inside the ring, wrap the wire twice around the ring. Repeat 11 times.

3 Cut an 8-in. (20 cm) piece of wire. Center the ring and wrap each end once around the ring.

4 On each end, string three crystals, curving them over the three crystals from steps 1 and 2. Wrap each end three times around the ring. Trim the excess wire and tuck the end.

5 Open a jump ring (Basics, p. 12) and attach the beaded ring and the loop of an earring post. Close the jump ring. Make a second earring.

Supplies

- **36** 3 mm round crystals
- **2** 20 mm hammered rings
- 40 in. (1 m) 28-gauge wire
- **2** 5 mm jump rings
- pair of earring posts and ear nuts
- **2** pairs of pliers
- diagonal wire cutters

Aquamarine sparkle

Connect a few crystals and pieces of fancy chain for a bib-style necklace

By Jane Konkel

The color of these pristine cubes remind me of pool water and are drilled diagonally, making them a shapely companion for floating rectangle chain.

1 On a head pin, string a 4 mm cube crystal and make the first half of a wrapped loop (Basics, p. 12). Cut two 3-in. (7.6 cm) pieces of wire. On one wire, make a wrapped loop. String a spacer, a 6 mm cube, and a spacer. Make a wrapped loop. On the other wire, make the first half of a wrapped loop. String an 8 mm cube and make the first half of a wrapped loop. Make six 4 mm units, five 6 mm units, and five 8 mm units.

2 Attach the loop of a 4 mm unit to a loop of a 6 mm unit. Complete the wraps. Attach the remaining loop of the 6 mm unit and a loop of an 8 mm unit and complete the wraps. Leave the top loop unwrapped. Make five crystal dangles.

3 Cut a 1¾-in. (4.4 cm), two 1-in. (2.5 cm), and two ½-in. (1.3 cm) pieces of floating rectangle chain. Attach the unwrapped loop of a dangle and an end round link of a chain. Complete the wraps. Attach each of the remaining dangles and a piece of chain.

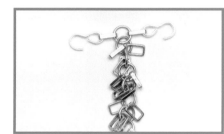

Supplies

- **5** 8 mm cube crystals, diagonally drilled
- **5** 6 mm cube crystals, diagonally drilled
- **6** 4 mm cube crystals, diagonally drilled
- **10** 4 mm flat spacers
- 30 in. (76 cm) 22-gauge wire
- 10–14 in. (25–36 cm) box chain, 3 mm links
- 5 in. (13 cm) floating rectangle chain, 5 mm links
- **8** 9 mm Quick Links connectors
- **6** 1½-in. (3.8 cm) head pins
- **2** 5 mm jump rings
- lobster claw clasp and soldered jump ring or link
- chainnose and roundnose pliers
- diagonal wire cutters

4 Separate the pair of rectangles on the top link of the longest chain dangle.

Attach a Quick Links connector and one of the rectangles. Use chainnose pliers to close the attached half of the connector. Attach another connector and the remaining rectangle.

5 On each end, continue attaching rectangle links and connectors, closing each half of the connector as you go. Do not close the last half of the connector on each end.

6 Cut two 5–7-in. (13–18 cm) pieces of box chain. On each end of the beaded section, attach the connector and an end link of box chain. Close the connectors.

7 Open two jump rings (Basics, p. 12). Attach a connector and a lobster claw clasp. Close the jump rings. On the other end, use a connector to attach a soldered jump ring and the chain. Attach a 4 mm bead unit to the jump ring and complete the wraps.

Combine sequins with spacers and beads to change up the design.

Dream
sequins

Link vintage sparklers for a retro look

by Suzanne Branca

I am always looking for lightweight earrings that feel good all day. This design is a dream come true: light as a feather with a big, sparkly feel. You can make them with all sorts of different colors and shapes of sequins. The choices are limitless.

1 Open a jump ring (Basics, p. 12). Attach an open-square sequin, an oval sequin, and a square. Close the jump ring. Make five three-sequin units.

2 Open the jump ring of a three-sequin unit. Attach a square and close the jump ring. Use a jump ring to attach a second square.

Cut a two-link piece of chain. Use a jump ring to attach the dangle to the chain.

Supplies

- ◆ **10** 12 mm oval sequins
- ◆ **24** 6 mm open-square sequins
- ◆ ¾ in. (1.9 cm) rectangle box chain, 3 mm links
- ◆ **14** 5 mm jump rings
- ◆ pair of lever-back earring wires
- ◆ **2** pairs of pliers (may include chainnose, roundnose, or bentnose)
- ◆ diagonal wire cutters

3 Attach two three-sequin units to each jump ring added in step 2.

4 Open the loop of an earring wire (Basics, p. 12). Attach the dangle and close the loop. Make a second earring.

Flower
ring

Fill a flower with sparkling crystals

By Kristal Wick

Top a silver ring band with a garnet-hued lampworked flower and fill the flower's center with bicone crystal stamens in coordinating colors. Wrapped wire secures the flower while the coils echo the swirls in the ring's band.

1 On a head pin, string a bicone crystal and make a wrapped loop (Basics, p. 12). Make eight bead units.

2 Cut a 7-in. (18 cm) piece of wire. String one hole of the button, the bead units, and the other hole of the button. Center the beads.

Supplies

- 22 mm glass flower button, with two holes
- **8** 4 mm bicone crystals, in three colors
- 7 in. (18 cm) 22-gauge dead-soft wire
- **8** 1½-in. (3.8 cm) head pins
- ring band
- chainnose and roundnose pliers
- diagonal wire cutters

Flower button from Unicorne Beads, unicornebeads.com.

3 Wrap each end of the wire twice around the band in opposite directions.

4 On each end of the wire, use the tip of your roundnose pliers to make a small loop. Use chainnose pliers to form a 4 mm coil.

Tip

Use two pairs of pliers to grasp each coil as you wrap the wire in step 5.

5 Wrap each end snugly around the wire between the flower and band. Flatten each coil against the band on each side of the flower.

Metal

& Chain

BIB in BLOOM

Drape chain and metal flowers in a statement necklace

by Naomi Fujimoto

Before cutting each piece of chain, try the necklace on to check the drape.

There's never been a better time to be a flower girl; the trend is going strong. Try a variety of different elements: I used brass and gold-plated flowers with silver-backed cup chain — plus dots of orange — for a mix-and-match effect. An off-center bracelet dangle and smaller lily pad earrings continue the flower theme without overdoing it.

1 necklace • On a head pin, string a margarita crystal, the center of a flower, and a spacer. Make a right-angle bend. Wrap the head pin wire around the stem, between the spacer and flower. Trim the excess wire.

2a Apply glue to a flat-back crystal. Use chainnose pliers to place the flat back on the center of a flower. Allow to dry.

b Attach margaritas, as in step 1, or flat backs, as in step 2a, to make five flower units.

3 Open a 7 mm (medium) jump ring (Basics, p. 12). Attach a petal of a flower unit and a petal of a second flower unit. Close the jump ring. Use medium jump rings to attach the remaining flower units.

4 Cut two 4½–6-in. (11.4–15 cm) pieces of 8 mm link chain. Attach one end of each chain to a 12–13 mm (large) jump ring. Use medium jump rings to attach each end of the flower section to a large jump ring.

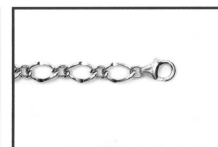

5 Use a 4 mm (small) jump ring to attach a lobster claw clasp and the remaining end of one chain from step 4.

6 On a head pin, string an 8 mm round crystal, a margarita, and a spacer. Make the first half of a wrapped loop (Basics, p. 12). Attach the other end of the chain and complete the wraps.

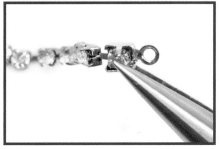

7 Place one end of a cup chain in a cup connector. Use chainnose pliers to fold over the prongs.

8 Attach the loop of the cup connector to one of the large jump rings. Trim the chain to the desired length. Attach a cup connector to the cut end, then attach the other large jump ring.

back view

9 Attach chains as desired; check the drape as you go. I attached chains in the following lengths: 6 in. (15 cm) cup chain, 7 in. (18 cm) 8 mm chain, 7½ in. (19.1 cm) cup chain, 9 in. (23 cm) 8 mm chain, 10 in. (25 cm) cup chain.

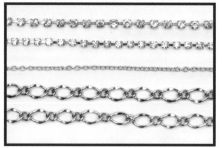

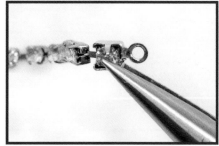

1 bracelet • Following steps 1 or 2a of the necklace, make a flower unit.

2 Decide how long you want your bracelet to be, subtract ½ in. (1.3 cm), and cut two cup chains, one 2–3 mm link chain, and two 8 mm link chains to that length.

3 Place one end of a cup chain in a cup connector. Use chain-nose pliers to fold over the prongs. Repeat on the other end. Attach cup connectors to each end of the second piece of cup chain.

4 Open a jump ring (Basics, p. 12). Attach the loop of a cup connector, an end link of 8 mm chain, and an outer loop of half of a slide clasp. Close the jump ring. Repeat with the remaining cup chain and 8 mm chain. Use jump rings to attach the other chain ends and clasp half.

5 Use jump rings to attach the 2–3 mm chain and the center loop of each half of the clasp.

6 Use a jump ring to attach the flower unit to one of the outer chains.

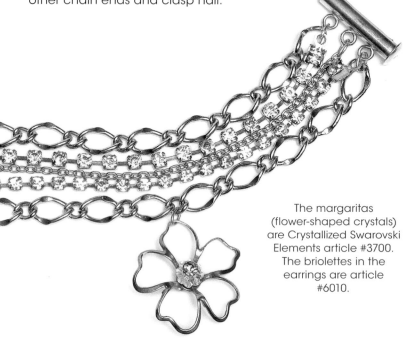

The margaritas (flower-shaped crystals) are Crystallized Swarovski Elements article #3700. The briolettes in the earrings are article #6010.

Attaching chain

- You can use a neck form or bust to help you check the drape of the necklace.
- Use additional 7 mm jump rings to attach the chains (or flowers) if they drape better that way.

1 earrings • Open a jump ring (Basics, p. 12). Attach a briolette and a loop of a lily pad bloom. Close the jump ring.

2 Open the loop of an earring wire (Basics, p. 12). Attach the dangle and close the loop. Make a second earring.

Supplies

necklace 16 in. (41 cm)
- 75 mm metal flower
- 55 mm brass flower
- **2** 35 mm metal eight-petal flowers
- 26 mm metal three-petal clover flower
- 16 mm metal lily pad bloom
- 8 mm round crystal
- **3–4** 6–10 mm margarita crystals
- **2–3** 6–8 mm flat-back crystals
- **3–4** 3–4 mm spacers
- 25–36 in. (64–91 cm) chain, 8 mm links
- 16–21 in. (41–53 cm) 2.5–3 mm cup chain, color A
- 7½–9 in. (19.1–23 cm) 2.5–3 mm cup chain, color B
- **6** cup connectors
- **3–4** 1½-in. (3.8 cm) head pins
- **2** 12–13 mm (large) jump rings
- **7–17** 7 mm (medium) jump rings
- 4 mm (small) jump ring
- lobster claw clasp
- chainnose and roundnose pliers
- diagonal wire cutters
- Gem-Tac

bracelet
- 25 mm metal shamrock flower
- 5–6 mm flat crystal, center drilled
- 3–4 mm spacer

- 12–16 in. (30–41 cm) chain, 8 mm links
- 6–8 in. (15–20 cm) chain, 2–3 mm links
- 12–16 in. (30–41 cm) 2.5–3 mm cup chain
- **4** cup connectors
- **1**½-in. (3.8 cm) decorative head pin
- **7** 4 mm jump rings
- three-strand slide clasp
- chainnose and roundnose pliers, or **2** pairs of chainnose pliers
- diagonal wire cutters

earrings
- **2** 21 mm crystal briolettes
- **2** 16 mm metal lily pad blooms
- **2** 7 mm jump rings
- pair of earring wires
- chainnose and roundnose pliers, or **2** pairs of chainnose pliers

Design alternative

Earrings aren't just a side note: Try different flower (or leaf) arrangements when a statement necklace is too much.

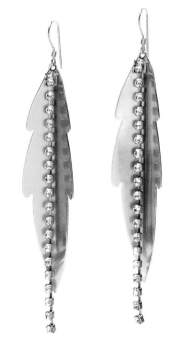

Supply note

For more delicate, lightweight earrings, use smaller briolettes. The crystal briolettes are also available in 11, 13, and 17 mm sizes. (You can even skip the beads altogether.)

1

bracelet • Make the components (p. 60). Open a 6 mm copper jump ring. Attach the bar half of a toggle clasp and a heart spacer. Close the jump ring. Attach another jump ring to the bar and spacer.

2

Use a pair of 8 mm jump rings to attach the spacer and a rivoli component. Attach a pair of 8 mm jump rings to the opposite side of the rivoli component.

3

To the pair of 8 mm jump rings, attach: pair of 6 mm jump rings, pair of 8 mm jump rings, oval link, pair of 8 mm jump rings, pair of 6 mm jump rings, pair of 10 mm jump rings, gear component.

> 66My favorite part of teaching is the exchange of ideas that happens so naturally when people are being creative.99
> –Irina

Making co

Jump rings get glamorous when they join beautiful components

by Irina Miech

I love showing my students how to turn ordinary supplies into something extraordinary. Jump rings generally don't elicit oohs and ahhs, but just look at the role they play in this bracelet. Get started by going through your supplies and pulling out items that can be linked together. Choose pieces with large holes, such as metal gears, filigrees, and spacers. Wire crystal pendants to a few of the components, then connect them with pairs of jump rings. Lesson learned? There are no unimportant findings, just unexplored possibilities.

4

To the gear component, attach: pair of 10 mm jump rings, pair of 6 mm jump rings, pair of 8 mm jump rings, leaf, pair of 8 mm jump rings, pair of 6 mm jump rings, pair of 8 mm jump rings, flat spacer.

5

To the flat spacer, attach: pair of 8 mm jump rings, pair of 6 mm jump rings, pair of 8 mm jump rings, cosmic crystal oval, pair of 8 mm jump rings, pair of 6 mm jump rings.

6

To the pair of 6 mm jump rings, use a 10 mm jump ring to attach a cosmic crystal pendant. Check the fit, and add or remove pairs of jump rings if necessary. Use a 10 mm jump ring to attach the loop half of the toggle clasp.

Finish the bracelet with a single crystal dangle.

nnections

earrings • Make two rivoli components (p. 60). Open an 8 mm gunmetal jump ring (Basics, p. 12) and attach a rivoli component. Close the jump ring.

1

2

Attach another 8 mm jump ring. Use a pair of 6 mm jump rings to attach the 8 mm jump rings and an earring wire. Make a second earring.

Components

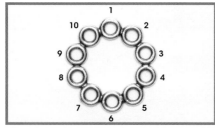

1 **a** rivoli component • Cut a 10-in. (25 cm) piece of wire. Wrap one end twice around the inside circle of ring 1 of a ten-ring circle component. Center a rivoli on the circle.

b Skipping two rings, string ring 4 front to back so the wire crosses the rivoli's edge.

c String the wire through ring 3, back to front.

2 Repeat steps 1b and c, skipping two rings each time, until you've gone all the way around, creating a pentagon.

Tip

To speed up the process of connecting jump rings, open all of them before beginning your bracelet.

3 **a** In back of the filigree, string the wire from ring 2 to ring 10, back to front.

b Skip two rings and string the wire through ring 3, front to back, so that it crosses the rivoli's edge.

c String the wire through ring 2, back to front.

d Repeat steps 3b and c, skipping two rings each time, until you have completed a pentagon.

e Wrap the wire around the inner side of a ring and trim the excess. Use chainnose pliers to tuck the end.

1 gear component • Cut two 4-in. (10 cm) pieces of wire. On opposite sides of the gear, wrap each wire three times around the gear.

2 In back of the gear, wrap each wire end around the wire wraps. Trim the excess and use chainnose pliers to tuck the ends.

Supplies

bracelet
- 15 mm cosmic crystal oval
- 14 mm cosmic crystal ring
- 14 mm crystal pendant
- 12 mm crystal rivoli
- 20 mm filigree leaf
- 19 mm gear component
- 16 mm circle component, with ten rings

- 15 mm oval link
- 9 mm large-hole flat spacer
- 9 mm large-hole heart spacer
- 18 in. (46 cm) 28-gauge wire
- **6** 10 mm copper jump rings
- **20–22** 8 mm gunmetal jump rings
- **14–16** 6 mm copper jump rings
- toggle clasp
- **2** pairs of pliers
- diagonal wire cutters

earrings
- **2** 12 mm crystal rivolis
- **2** 16 mm circle components, with ten rings
- 20 in. (51 cm) 28-gauge wire
- **4** 8 mm gunmetal jump rings
- **4** 6 mm copper jump rings
- pair of earring wires
- **2** pairs of pliers
- diagonal wire cutters

Give this bracelet an extra twist to make it smaller, or loosen up the twists for more length.

In the gold version, I made a 20-gauge wire clasp and strung it through the stitches on each end as in the labradorite version.

One stitch
Lots of style

Complex-looking wire crochet design is just a chain stitch

by Donna Weeks

After seeing many complicated jewelry designs in magazines, I decided to take the complication out of the process. I wanted an open and airy effect, and liked the idea of combining beads of different sizes, shapes, and finishes. Wire crochet made it happen.

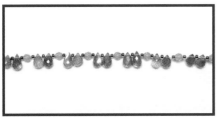

1 On the 28-gauge wire, string 16–22 in. (41–56 cm) of beads (Tips, p. 62).

2 About 6 in. (15 cm) from one end of the wire, make a loop. Bring the 6-in. (15 cm) tail behind the loop.

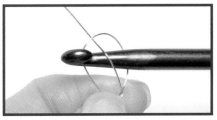

3 Insert a crochet needle under the tail and over the loop.

Supplies

- 16–22 in. (41–56 cm) assorted beads
- spool of 28-gauge dead-soft wire
- 6 in. (15 cm) 20-gauge half-hard wire
- chainnose and roundnose pliers
- diagonal wire cutters
- size H crochet needle
- nylon-jaw pliers (optional)

Tips

- You can use heavier gauge wire in your bracelet. I used 26-gauge wire for the labradorite version because I wanted more structure for the delicate teardrop beads and tiny 11° seed beads.
- The amount of wire you use will depend on the size and tension of your stitches, so it's best to string beads directly onto the wire coil (or spool) rather than cutting a piece of wire.
- The size of the beads will determine how many inches you string on the wire before you crochet. For instance, I strung 22 in. (56 cm) of beads for the pearl version (p. 63), but only 16 in. (41 cm) for the labradorite bracelet. It's easier to string too many beads in the beginning than to add them later.

4 Tighten the loop below the hook, leaving a little slack, to form a new loop around the needle.

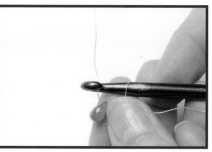

5 Slide a bead close to the crochet needle. Hook the wire above the bead.

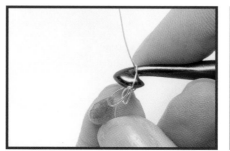

6 Pull the needle to bring the wire through the loop formed in step 4. This forms a new loop around the needle. Keep the loops loose enough to pull the needle through easily.

7 Slide another bead close to the crochet needle. Hook the wire above the bead and bring it through the loop created in step 6. Repeat until the crocheted strand can circle your wrist three times with 1 in. (2.5 cm) extra.

8 Cut the wire 6 in. (15 cm) from the last stitch. Fold the strand in thirds. There will be a fold and a wire tail on each end.

❝My designs always have to be something that can be completed within a two- to three-hour time frame.❞ —Donna

9 On each end, string the tail through a loop in the fold and pull tight. Wrap the wire around the loop a few times.

10 Twist the three segments together.

11 Cut a 3-in. (7.6 cm) piece of 20-gauge wire. Using roundnose pliers, make a small loop on one end.

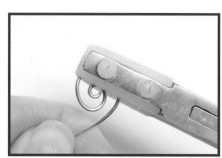

12 Use chainnose or nylon-jaw pliers and your fingers to shape a loose coil around the loop.

13 On the other end of the 20-gauge wire, make a tighter coil that faces the first coil to create a C shape. Make a second unit with coils in an S shape.

14 On each end, wrap each tail five or six times around the center of a coil unit. Trim the excess wire.

Design alternative

In the faux pearl version, the bead holes were large enough that I could string the 20-gauge wire through them. For extra stability, I strung the wire through several beads on each end before shaping the coils.

Twist a tree pendant

Wire wrap an ever-colorful focal piece

by Allyson Giesen

Remember those money trees they sold at trinket shops back in the day? I always loved them and wanted to incorporate the concept into jewelry. You can also interpret this pendant as the Tree of Life, an ancient symbol that has been used to represent everything from human origins to the connectedness of all life on earth. Choose colors in seasonal shades or play with the whole rainbow!

1 To make a hammered ring: Cut a 10-in. (25 cm) piece of 16-gauge wire and wrap it around a cylindrical object. Make a right-angle bend with one end and wrap the other end around it several times. Trim the wrapping wire. With the remaining end, make a plain loop (Basics, p. 12) perpendicular to the ring. Place the ring on a bench block or anvil. Hammer both sides of the ring.

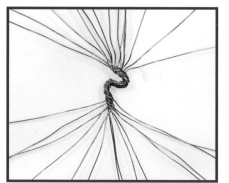

2 Cut 14 6-in. (15 cm) pieces of 26-gauge wire. Holding the wires in a bundle, begin twisting them together 1½ in. (3.8 cm) from one end. Twist for ½ in. (1.3 cm). Splay the wire ends above and below the twist. Use roundnose pliers to form two kinks in the twist.

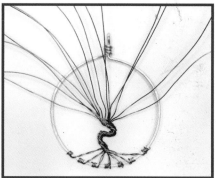

3 Place the bundle inside the ring with the short "root" wires at the bottom. Pinch together two adjacent root wires and twist them together loosely. Wrap both ends around the ring two or three times. Trim the excess wire and tuck the ends. Repeat with the remaining root wires.

With the tip of your roundnose pliers, kink the root wires.

The ring at left is from Beading Dreams; the ring at right was made following step 1.

Supplies

necklace 16 in. (41 cm)

- **150–175** 2–3 mm crystal, gemstone, cubic zirconia, or faceted glass round beads or rondelles
- 40–45 mm hammered ring, or 10 in. (25 cm) 16-gauge wire and cylindrical object
- 7 ft. (2.1 m) 26-gauge wire
- 16 in. (41 cm) chain, 2–5 mm links
- **2–3** 4–5 mm jump rings
- lobster claw clasp and soldered jump ring
- chainnose and roundnose pliers
- diagonal wire cutters
- bench block or anvil (optional)
- hammer (optional)

4 Pinch together two or three adjacent "branch" wires and twist them together two or three times. Separate the wires. On one wire, string enough 2–3 mm beads to reach the ring. Wrap the end around the ring, trim the excess wire, and tuck the end. Repeat with the remaining branch wires.

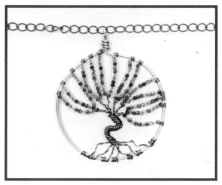

5 Cut a 16-in. (41 cm) piece of chain. If using a pre-made hammered ring, open a jump ring (Basics, p. 12) and attach the pendant and the center link of chain. Close the jump ring. If you made the ring, open the loop (Basics, p. 12), attach the center link of chain, and close the loop.

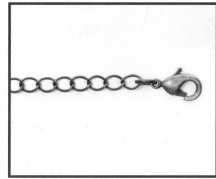

6 On one end of the chain, use a jump ring to attach a lobster claw clasp. Repeat on the other end, substituting a soldered jump ring for the clasp.

Transfer an image

Dress up a toggle for an asymmetrical lariat

by Mary Lynn Maloney

I wanted a warm, mixed-metal piece with the closure as part of the design, so I started with a bunch of different metal components. I kept the beads to a minimum to punctuate the graphic black floral imagery.

Include contrasting details, like a smooth toggle pendant with textured chains.

1 Cut an image from a transfer sheet to fit an oval toggle pendant. Soak the image in water for 40 seconds. Slide the filmy portion of the transfer onto the oval. Discard the backing and dab the image with a paper towel to remove the excess water.

2 Use a paintbrush to apply a thin coat of sealant over the entire pendant. Allow to dry. Apply a second coat and allow to dry.

3 On a head pin, string a 4–6 mm bead. Make a plain loop (Basics, p. 12). Make three bead units.

❝I really dig the dangly chain belts that were worn slung low on the hips of medieval gowns.❞ —Mary

Supplies

lariat 19 in. (48 cm)

- **3** 4–6 mm beads
- 16–20 in. (41–51 cm) chain, 9 mm links
- 13–17 in. (33–43 cm) chain, 5 mm links
- 2 in. (5 cm) chain, 3–4 mm links
- 17–21 in. (43 ~ 3 mm ~
- ~ ~ ~, 2–3 n. ~ ~ cm) head pins
- ~ ~ toggle pendant
- toggle ring
- twig connector
- twig toggle bar
- chainnose and roundnose pliers
- diagonal wire cutters
- paintbrush
- paper towels
- scissors
- sealant, such as Nunn Design Sealant
- transfer sheet
- water

Supplies from Nunn Designs (nunndesign.com).

4 Cut a 2-in. (5 cm) piece of 3–4 mm link chain. Open the loop of a bead unit (Basics, p. 13) and attach an end link. Close the loop. Repeat with a 3-in. (7.6 cm) and a 4-in. (10 cm) piece of 2–3 mm link chain.

5 Open the end link of the 2-in. (5 cm) chain. String the pendant's hole and attach another link of the chain. Close the link. Repeat with the remaining chains.

6 Cut a three-link piece of 9 mm link chain. Attach one end and the pendant's loop. Attach the other end and the small loop of a toggle ring.

7 Use a 9 mm link to attach the toggle ring and a loop of a twig connector. Cut a 14–18-in. (36–46 cm) piece of 9 mm link chain. Attach one end to the twig connector's other loop.

8 Cut a 13–17-in. (33–43 cm) piece of 5 mm link chain. Attach one end to the 9 mm chain near the connector.

9 Cut a 13–17-in. (33–43 cm) piece of 3 mm link chain. Attach one end to the 5 mm chain.

10 On the other end, attach the 3 mm chain to the 5 mm chain. Attach the 5 mm chain to the 9 mm chain. Attach the 9 mm chain to a twig toggle bar.

Design alternative

I used a "grande heart" and a ½-in. (1.3 cm) circle punch to punch images from a Paris collage sheet and a graphic florals transfer sheet. Before soaking the transfer sheet, tear the image on a diagonal; a ragged edge gives your piece more dimension. I used Gel du Soleil UV resin to fill the pendant.

Whether you prefer monochromes or brights, layer metal flowers for easy holiday decorations.

Fast, fabulous

Mix Lucite and metal flowers for gift-worthy baubles

by Naomi Fujimoto

1 small gold ornament • Open the loop of an eye pin (Basics, p. 12). Attach the loops of three 8 mm wired beads and close the loop.

Adapt flowers for a festive, fresh holiday project that's beautiful all year-round. Shades of purple, look pretty with either gold or silver. This project couldn't be simpler: Just make sure to string at least one flower that has holes in its outer petals so there's a place to attach chain. For a fun detail, try chain in a color to match.

flower ornaments

2 On the eye pin, string four to six wired beads, a three-petal flower, the center of a metal flower, and a spacer.

3 Bend the head pin wire next to the spacer and make a set of wraps between the spacer and the flower. Trim the excess wire.

4 Cut a 7–9-in. (18–23 cm) piece of chain. Open a jump ring (Basics, p. 12). Attach each end of the chain and one of the petals of the metal flower. Close the jump ring.

1 large silver ornament • Cut a 7–9-in. (18–23 cm) piece of chain. Open a jump ring (Basics, p. 12). Attach each end of the chain and a plastic filigree. Close the jump ring.

2 On a head pin, string seven to 11 wired beads, the center of the filigree, a metal flower, and a spacer.

Supplies

small gold ornament

- ◆ 72 mm metal flower
- ◆ 28 mm three-petal flower
- ◆ **7–9** 8–12 mm wired beads
- ◆ 4–5 mm spacer
- ◆ 7–9 in. (18–23 cm) chain, 4–6 mm links
- ◆ 2-in. (5 cm) eye pin
- ◆ **1–2** 4–6 mm jump rings
- ◆ chainnose and roundnose pliers
- ◆ diagonal wire cutters

large silver ornament

- ◆ 4-in. (10 cm) metal magnolia flower
- ◆ 30 mm plastic filigree
- ◆ **7–11** 8–35 mm wired beads
- ◆ 4–5 mm spacer
- ◆ 7–9 in. (18–23 cm) chain, 3–4 mm links
- ◆ 2½-in. (6.4 cm) decorative head pin
- ◆ **1–2** 4–6 mm jump rings
- ◆ chainnose and roundnose pliers
- ◆ diagonal wire cutters

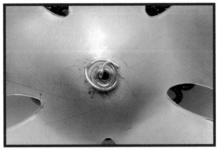

3 Bend the head pin wire next to the spacer and make a set of wraps between the spacer and the flower. Trim the excess wire.

Design alternative

I layered a couple of Lucite flowers and set them in a ring bezel with Ice Resin.

Tips

- • To change the direction your ornament hangs, use a second jump ring to attach the chain ends to the first jump ring.
- • When you wrap the head pin wire next to the spacer, use chainnose or crimping pliers to tuck and tighten the wraps.

- • Store the ornaments wrapped in tissue paper to keep them from getting scratched.

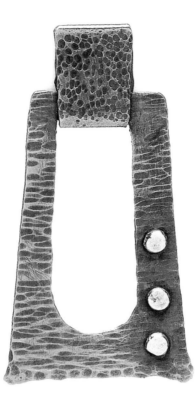

No-solder
metal
earrings

Give basic
metalworking a
try for striking
geometric earrings

by Kim St. Jean

I love working with metals and using cold-connection techniques (no soldering). These earrings incorporate a variety of metalworking skills — cutting, piercing, texturing, folding, and riveting. Every time I teach a class, I learn something new from my students' questions and the issues they raise. The most important thing I try to teach them is that a class is about learning the skills, not making a perfect piece of jewelry. But with a little practice, you'll surprise yourself with the beautiful things you create.

Supplies

- 24-gauge copper sheet
- **6** rivets
- pair of earring post pads with ear nuts
- bench pin
- flatnose pliers
- ball peen hammer
- texture hammers
- bench block or anvil
- jeweler's saw with 3/0 blades
- metal file
- metal punch
- shears
- fine-point felt tip pen
- liver of sulfur (optional)

Tips

- For the photos, I used a single texture hammer with interchangeable heads. You can also buy copper sheeting that's already textured on one side. If you use textured sheeting, skip step 7.
- I used premade rivets to demonstrate the project, but I usually make my own rivets by balling the end of 16-gauge wire with a torch.
- It's a good idea to have extra saw blades on hand, especially if you're new to sawing.

Videos

There are several helpful videos at ArtJewelryMag.com/videos for metalwork novices:

- Threading a saw blade in a saw frame
- Piercing metal
- Balling the end of wire
- Liver of sulfur patina

1 For each earring: Use shears to cut a 1 x 1½-in. (2.5 x 3.8 cm) copper rectangle. At the top of the rectangle, mark ⅛ in. (3 mm) from each side. Cut from the bottom corners along the lines.

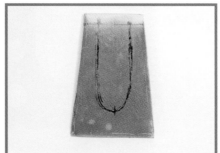

2 Draw a line ⅛ in. (3 mm) from the top. Mark ³⁄₁₆ in. (5 mm) from each side. Mark 1 in. (2.5 cm) down from the center of the line. Draw a U connecting the points.

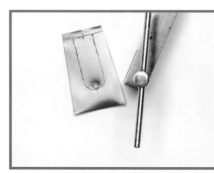

3 Use a metal punch to punch a hole at the bottom of the U.

4 Unfasten one side of the blade from a saw and insert it in the hole. Re-fasten the blade (Videos).

5 Attach the bench pin (a wooden extension made for sawing and filing) to the work surface and position the saw blade in the V (obscured by my thumb in the photo). Saw along the U, stopping at the top line (Videos).

6 With your flatnose pliers, fold the U-shaped flap up at a right angle. File and shape the edges as needed.

7 On a bench block or anvil, use a texture hammer to texture the outer part of the copper. Texture a different pattern on the flap that faces the outer textured surface.

8 Fold the flap back about ½ in. (1.3 cm) from the first fold. Punch a hole for the earring post about ⅛ in. (3 mm) from the fold.

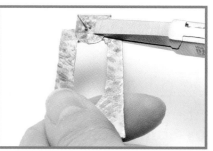

9 Insert the earring post and use chainnose pliers to flatten the flap. Trim the flap if it overlaps the U-shaped hole.

10 Mark and punch three holes on one side of the U.

11 Insert a rivet in each hole. Use the flat end of a ball-peen hammer to strike the back of the rivet squarely to flatten the end. Add a patina with liver of sulfur if desired (Videos).

Design note

I experimented with a "no saw" option and used shears to pierce the U design. It's possible, but it wasn't pretty. This method was much more time consuming (tiny snips, much more filing) and still didn't look quite right. I'd recommend trying a saw — just practice on scrap metal first.

Ball-chain hoops

Do a little wire wrapping for quick earrings

by Sonia Kumar

I love to find an unexpected use for interesting materials. "What can I do with this?" is always the first question I ask myself when I'm designing a new piece. I had a couple of short pieces of ball chain lying around and I knew that just throwing them away was not the answer (is it ever?).

Supplies
- **2** 6 mm round beads
- 5–6 in. (13–15 cm) ball chain
- memory wire, ring diameter
- 12 in. (30 cm) 24-gauge wire
- **2** 1½-in. (3.8 cm) head pins
- **2** 7 mm jump rings
- pair of earring wires
- chainnose and roundnose pliers
- diagonal wire cutters
- heavy-duty wire cutters

1 Use heavy-duty wire cutters to cut one complete ring from a memory wire coil. If you don't have heavy-duty wire cutters, grip the wire with chainnose pliers and bend it back and forth until it breaks. Never use jewelry-weight cutters on memory wire.

2 Wrap a piece of ball chain around the outside of the memory wire and trim to fit.

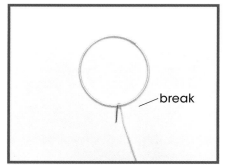

3 Cut a 6-in. (15 cm) piece of 24-gauge wire and wrap one end around the memory wire two or three times across from the break in the memory wire.

4 Wrap the 24-gauge wire around the chain between the first two balls and around the memory wire.

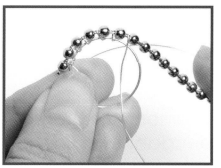

5 Continue wrapping the 24-gauge wire between the balls and around the memory wire until you reach the end of the chain.

6 Wrap the 24-gauge wire once around the memory wire and trim the excess wire.

7 On a head pin, string a bead and make a plain loop (Basics, p. 12).

8 Open a jump ring (Basics, p 12). Attach the loop of an earring wire, the hoop, and the bead unit. Close the jump ring. Make a second earring.

Tip
Try bracelet-diameter memory wire for large statement hoops.

Any shape bead can be used in the center, but echoing the round hoop creates a calming symmetry.

Create a necklace o

Connect a textured pendant and links for a fresh necklace and earrings

by Leah Rivers

René Lalique, my favorite artist, designed jewelry that shifted away from precious gemstones and towards more realistic forms based on nature. The silver branch pendant and links in my necklace and earrings are inspired by the roots of an ancient pine in one of his fabulous pendants. This set has a moody feel, with lots of energy in the twisted branches.

Bead units

briolette unit • Cut a 5-in. (13 cm) piece of wire. String a briolette and make a set of wraps above it (Basics, p. 12). Using the largest part of your roundnose pliers, make the first half of a wrapped loop (Basics, p. 12) perpendicular to the briolette.

head pin unit • On a decorative head pin, string a rondelle and a spacer. Using the largest part of your roundnose pliers, make the first half of a wrapped loop Make three head pin units.

small-loop unit • Cut a 2½-in. (6.4 cm) piece of wire. Make the first half of a wrapped loop. String a spacer, a rondelle, and a spacer. Make the first half of a wrapped loop. Make two small-loop units.

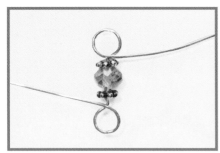

large-loop unit • Cut a 3½-in. (8.9 cm) piece of wire. Using the largest part of your roundnose pliers, make the first half of a wrapped loop. String a spacer, a rondelle, and a spacer. Make the first half of a large wrapped loop. Make six large-loop units.

perpendicular-loop unit • Cut a 3-in. (7.6 cm) piece of wire. Make the first half of a wrapped loop. String a spacer, a rondelle, and a spacer. Using the largest part of your roundnose pliers, make the first half of a wrapped loop perpendicular to the first. Make two perpendicular-loop units.

❝I wanted to experiment with all the different places dangles could be attached to this organic centerpiece, yet still keep the focus on the movement in the twisted organic shapes of the branches.❞ —Leah

natural wonders

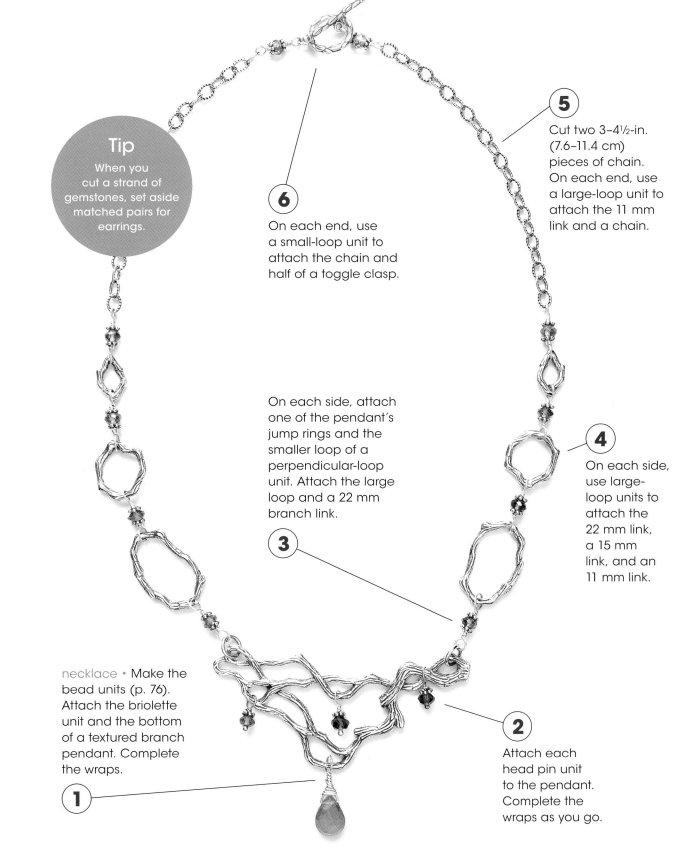

Tip

When you cut a strand of gemstones, set aside matched pairs for earrings.

6 On each end, use a small-loop unit to attach the chain and half of a toggle clasp.

5 Cut two 3–4½-in. (7.6–11.4 cm) pieces of chain. On each end, use a large-loop unit to attach the 11 mm link and a chain.

On each side, attach one of the pendant's jump rings and the smaller loop of a perpendicular-loop unit. Attach the large loop and a 22 mm branch link.

3

4 On each side, use large-loop units to attach the 22 mm link, a 15 mm link, and an 11 mm link.

necklace • Make the bead units (p. 76). Attach the briolette unit and the bottom of a textured branch pendant. Complete the wraps.

1

2 Attach each head pin unit to the pendant. Complete the wraps as you go.

Supplies

necklace 17 in. (43 cm)
- 63 mm textured branch pendant with two jump rings
- **2** 22 mm textured branch links
- **2** 15 mm textured branch links
- **2** 11 mm textured branch links
- 7–9 mm briolette
- **13** 4 mm faceted rondelles
- **23** 3–4 mm daisy spacers
- 37 in. (94 cm) 24-gauge wire
- 6–9 in. (15–23 cm) textured cable chain, 4 mm links
- **3** 1½-in. (3.8 cm) decorative head pins
- toggle clasp
- chainnose and roundnose pliers
- diagonal wire cutters

earrings
- **2** 24 mm textured branch links
- **2** 7–9 mm briolettes
- **2** 4 mm faceted rondelles
- **2** 3–4 mm daisy spacers
- 14 in. (36 cm) 24-gauge wire
- pair of textured earring wires
- chainnose and roundnose pliers
- diagonal wire cutters

3 Attach the large loop to the briolette unit and a branch link. Attach the dangle and the loop of an earring wire. Complete the wraps as you go. Make a second earring.

2 Make a perpendicular-loop unit (p. 76), omitting the top spacer.

1 Cut a 4-in. (10 cm) piece of wire. String a briolette and make a set of wraps above it (Basics, p. 12). Make a wrapped loop (Basics, p. 12), extending the wraps toward the briolette.

Design alternative

Textured components give these earrings an organic, handwrought style.

Connect
large links
and
leaves

Add sparkle to your fall wardrobe with an easy chain necklace

by Beki Haley

You can also try antiqued-brass or gunmetal chain with jewel-toned crystals.

Crisp, cool air and the stunning colors of autumn inspired this gorgeous necklace. Because the chain has large links, it won't take much time to make your own version. The necklace is versatile, too: Wear it extra long or wrap it a few times. Either way, you'll have lots of options if your style moods change faster than the seasons.

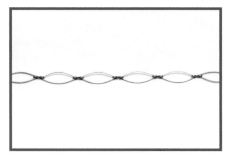

1 necklace • On an eye pin, string: 3 mm spacer, 4 mm bicone crystal, 4 mm spacer, 8 mm bicone crystal, 4 mm spacer, 4 mm bicone, 3 mm spacer. Make a plain loop (Basics, p. 12). Make nine or 10 connector units.

2 On a head pin, string: 3 mm spacer, 4 mm bicone, 4 mm spacer, 8 mm bicone, 4 mm spacer. Make a plain loop. Make eight or nine dangles.

3 Cut nine or 10 six-link pieces of chain.

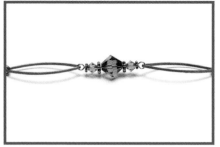

4 Open a loop of a connector unit (Basics, p. 12) and attach an end link of chain. Close the loop. Attach the other loop and a chain. Use connector units to attach the remaining pieces of chain, attaching the last connector unit to the first piece of chain.

5 On one chain segment, between the third and fourth marquise links, attach a dangle to one of the small links. Repeat until you've attached all of the dangles. (One chain segment will not have a dangle attached.)

6 Open a jump ring (Basics, p. 12). Attach a leaf to one of the small links between the third and fourth marquise links. Close the jump ring. Attach the remaining leaves as desired.

1 earrings • On a head pin, string: 3 mm spacer, 4 mm bicone crystal, 4 mm spacer, 8 mm bicone crystal, 4 mm spacer. Make a plain loop (Basics, p. 12).

2 Open the loop of an earring wire (Basics, p. 12). Attach the dangle and close the loop. Make a second earring.

Supplies

necklace 76 in. (1.9 m)

- **3** 40–60 mm leaves
- **17–19** 8 mm bicone crystals
- **26–29** 4 mm bicone crystals
- **34–38** 4 mm flat spacers
- **26–29** 3 mm flat spacers
- **6–7** ft. (1.8–2.1 m) marquise-link chain, 27 mm links
- **7–8** 1½-in. (3.8 cm) head pins
- **10–11** 1½-in. (3.8 cm) eye pins
- **3** 4–5 mm jump rings
- chainnose and roundnose pliers
- diagonal wire cutters

earrings

- **2** 8 mm bicone crystals
- **2** 4 mm bicone crystals
- **4** 4 mm flat spacers
- **2** 3 mm flat spacers
- **2** 1½-in. (3.8 cm) head pins
- pair of earring wires
- chainnose and roundnose pliers
- diagonal wire cutters

Supply notes

Here are the crystal colors I used in the necklace:

8 mm bicones
  2 amethyst
  3 crystal golden shadow
  3 olivine
  3 padparadscha
  3 tanzanite
  3 topaz

4 mm bicones
  5 amethyst
  2 crystal golden shadow
  7 olivine
  4 padparadscha
  4 tanzanite
  4 topaz

In the earrings, I used 8 mm topaz and 4 mm tanzanite bicones.

❝Don't be too judgmental of your art. You're starting the process with something that is already beautiful — the beads.**❞** –Beki

Tip
Use twist ties to check the placement of the leaves on the chain before attaching them.

Design alternative

If you want to play up the leaf theme a bit more, make a bracelet with smaller leaves in different finishes.

RIVETING necklace

Join brass components for multilayered steampunk style

by Jess Italia Lincoln

I love the movement and industrial feel of the steampunk components in my *Time Traveler* necklace. I used Vintaj brass and Arte Metal components and tied the design together with a handmade textured ceramic heart. To add a splash of color, I painted and inked brass charms and introduced multitoned Czech glass beads into the design.

Steampunk components

head pin unit • On a head pin, string an oval bead. Make a plain loop (Basics, p. 12).

eye pin unit • On an eye pin, string a coin bead. Make a plain loop (Basics, p. 12). Make three eye pin units with coin beads and two eye pin units with oval beads.

1 keyhole unit • Center a rectangle jump ring on a keyhole decorivet.

2 Bend the prongs around the rectangle. Make two keyhole units.

1 paint/ink charms • Dab acrylic paint on a charm. Allow to dry.

2 Apply alcohol ink to the charm and allow to dry. On the clock charm, use a file, emery board, or sandpaper to remove some color from the hands and numbers.

Tips

- If you prefer the clasp in the front, you can turn the heart and key into a working toggle and eliminate the hook-and-chain closure in the back.
- You can connect components to the gears and plate using brads in place of rivets. Simply stack the findings and gear on a brad then flatten the points along the back to secure.

1 necklace • Make the steampunk components (pp. 82 and 84). Attach the components in the following steps using 7 mm jump rings unless otherwise noted.

2 Cut a seven-link piece of elongated-oval chain. Open the loop of the head pin unit (Basics, p. 12) and attach an end link. Close the loop.

3 Attach an eye pin unit to the other end of the chain.

13 Attach an eye pin unit and a right-angle connector unit.

14 Attach a hook clasp.

4 Attach a triangle jump ring. Use a 5 mm jump ring to attach the secret key charm to the triangle.

5 Use an etched jump ring to attach an oval-plate unit.

12 Attach a spoked-gear unit and a keyhole unit.

Attach an eye pin unit. Punch a hole on one side of the curvature unit and use an etched jump ring to attach the eye pin unit.

6 Attach an eye pin unit and a clock-hands unit.

11 Use 5 mm jump rings to attach a clock charm and a heart charm to the triangle.

8

7 Attach a keyhole unit.

10 Attach an eye pin unit. Use etched jump rings to attach a hinge and a triangle jump ring.

9 Attach a 15 mm jump ring. Use a 10 mm jump ring to attach a skeleton key and a ceramic heart to the 15 mm jump ring. Attach cable chain to the skeleton key and heart as shown below.

More components

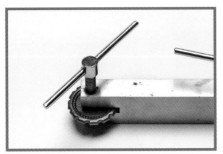

1 To assemble a riveted component • When necessary, use a hole punch to make a hole in the base component.

2 On a rivet, stack the desired components.

3 Using heavy-duty wire cutters, trim the rivet to 2 mm.

4 Place the stacked components on a bench block or anvil. With a chasing hammer, strike the rivet squarely to flatten the end. Make one of each unit shown on next page:

Supply notes

- The gearwheels, right-angle connectors, and curvature are from the Vintaj "Odd Parts" Fastenables set.
- The spoked gears, clock hands, and clock charm are from the Vintaj "Clockworks" set.
- The keyhole deco-rivets are from the "Navigation" Arte Metal decorivets set.
- The hinge is from the "Bric-A-Brac" Arte Metal hardware set.
- The oval plate is from the "Plates" Arte Metal hardware set.
- You can purchase individual components at Beadaholique, beadaholique.com.

Supplies

necklace 17 in. (43 cm)
- 50 mm ceramic heart
- 43 mm skeleton key
- 42 x 14 mm hinge
- 35 mm clock-hand connector
- 34 mm oval four-hole plate
- 29 mm curvature
- 23 mm secret key charm
- **2** 22 mm spoked gears
- 20 mm open gearwheel
- **2** 20 mm gearwheels
- 20 mm clock hands
- 20 mm clock charm
- 15 mm heart charm
- **2** 15 mm round keyhole decorivets
- **3** 12 mm Czech glass puffed oval beads
- **3** 10 mm Czech glass puffed coin beads

- **2** 10 mm standard washers
- **6** 9 mm daisy washers
- **2** 5 mm right-angle connectors
- 2½ in. (6.4 cm) elongated-oval chain, 11.5 mm links
- 1 in. (2.5 cm) cable chain, 4 mm links
- **6** ¼-in. (6 mm) nail-head rivets
- 1-in. (2.5 cm) head pin
- **5** 1-in. (2.5 cm) eye pins
- **2** 25 mm triangle jump rings
- **2** 23 mm rectangle jump rings
- 15 mm jump ring
- 10 mm jump ring
- **4** 9 mm etched jump rings
- **16** 7 mm jump rings
- **2** 5 mm jump rings
- hook clasp
- chainnose and roundnose pliers

- diagonal wire cutters
- heavy-duty wire cutters
- bench block or anvil
- chasing hammer
- metal hole punch
- nail file, emery board, or fine sandpaper
- sponge paintbrush
- Adirondack Acrylic Paint Dabbers (copper and pool)
- Adirondack Alcohol Inks (rust and stream)

Ceramic Heart from Earthenwood Studio, earthenwood.etsy.com.

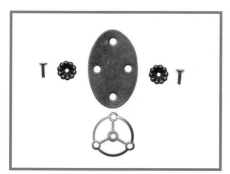

oval-plate unit • Open gearwheel, oval plate, two daisy washers, two rivets.

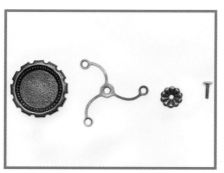

curvature unit • Spoked gear, curvature, daisy washer, rivet.

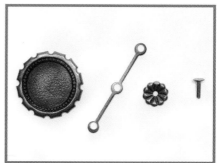

spoked-gear unit • Spoked gear, clock-hand connector, daisy washer, rivet.

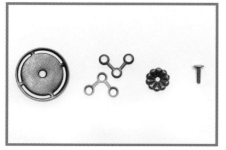

right-angle connector unit • Gearwheel, two right-angle connectors, daisy washer, standard washer (optional, not shown), rivet.

clock-hands unit • Gearwheel, clock hands, daisy washer, standard washer (optional, not shown), rivet. Add a standard washer if the hole of the base component is significantly larger than the rivet.

Design alternatives

Experiment with other riveting, painting, and inking options.

Gears in
BLOOM

Build gears with enameled flowers

by Irina Miech

When I hear *steampunk*, watch parts, keys, and gears usually come to mind. Flowers are an unlikely addition, but I couldn't resist pairing C-Koop's enameled flowers with copper gears. The technique to make this necklace and earrings is easy; just use head pins and jump rings to connect these playful metal components.

1 necklace • On four ball-end head pins, string a spacer, a 21 mm flower, and a 25 mm sectioned gear.

2 Separate the head pins into pairs. Wrap each pair around the gear and the head pins' stems to attach the components. Make three flower-and-gear units.

3 Open a pair of jump rings (Basics, p. 12). On one side of a flower-and-gear unit, use the pair of jump rings to attach a 16 mm open gear. Close the jump rings. On the other side of the unit, use a second pair of jump rings to attach a 16 mm sectioned gear.

4 Use pairs of jump rings to attach the remaining gears and flower-and-gear units.

5 Cut two 6–7-in. (15–18 cm) pieces of chain. On each end of the flower-and-gear section, use a jump ring to attach a piece of chain.

Supplies

necklace 22 in. (56 cm)
- 26 mm four-petal flower
- 21 mm five-petal flower
- 15 mm five-petal flower
- 25 mm sectioned gear
- **2** 19 mm sectioned gears
- **2** 16 mm sectioned gears
- **2** 16 mm open gears
- **6** 5 mm flat spacers
- 12–14 in. (30–36 cm) chain, 3–4 mm links
- **13** 2½-in. (6.4 cm) ball-end head pins
- **20–24** 9 mm jump rings
- lobster claw clasp
- chainnose and roundnose pliers
- diagonal wire cutters

earrings
- **2** 15 mm five-petal flowers
- **2** 19 mm sectioned gears
- **2** 5 mm flat spacers
- **6** 2½-in. (6.4 cm) ball-end head pins
- **2** 9 mm jump rings
- **4** 6 mm jump rings
- pair of earring wires
- **2** pairs of pliers
- diagonal wire cutters

Enameled flower and gear components by C-Koop Beads

6 On one end, use a jump ring to attach a lobster claw clasp.

7 On a ball-end head pin, string three spacers and make a wrapped loop (Basics, p. 12). Attach six to eight jump rings and the remaining chain to make an extender. Attach the dangle to the last jump ring.

1 earrings • On three ball-end head pins, string a spacer, a flower, and a sectioned gear.
Separate the head pins. Wrap each around the gear and the head pin stem to attach the components.

2 Open two 6 mm jump rings (Basics, p. 12) and attach the flower-and-gear unit to a 9 mm jump ring. Close the jump rings.

3 Open the loop of an earring wire (Basics, p. 12). Attach the dangle and close the loop. Make a second earring.

"Steampunk is a wonderful juxtaposition of Victorian culture, science fiction, and fantasy." —Irina

Apply ink, then remove some to accent the scrolls in a frame.

Design a metal
masterpiece

Transform a blank brass canvas into a mini work of art

by Jess Italia Lincoln

Cut, file, texture. Transfer an image, imprint text, set rivets — this project is a jewelry artist's dream! (And it's deceptively easy.) You can further embellish your piece with a few beads and subtle brass findings. You'll have so much fun making your metal masterpiece, you may find yourself creating an entire collection.

1 pendant • Use metal snips to cut a 1½ x ¾-in. (3.8 x 1.9 cm) rectangle from the canvas. Trim and round off the corners with a metal file.

2 Mark the center on the top and bottom of the frame. Use the smaller hole of a two-hole punch or hole-punch pliers to make two holes.

3 Use the holes in the frame as a guide to mark holes on the canvas. Punch two holes in the canvas.

4 Follow the package instructions to transfer an image onto the canvas. On a bench block, hammer letter stamps to imprint text on the canvas with a jeweler's hammer.

5 Use brass plates, texture hammers, or metal decorative stamps to add texture to canvas.

6 Dab acrylic paint on the frame and the canvas. Remove the excess paint from the canvas with a paper towel, leaving some paint to accentuate the text. Apply alcohol ink to both pieces. Allow to dry. Apply a sealer if desired.

7 On a rivet, stack the frame on the canvas. Use a chasing hammer to strike the rivet squarely to flatten the end. Repeat with another rivet.

Cutting
Safety first: Wear goggles and a paper mask over your mouth and nose when cutting and filing.

Filing
Conserve energy by filing in one direction.

> **"It's wonderful to see everyone's personal style come out in the altered techniques classes that I teach."** —Jess

1 necklace • On a head pin, string a pearl and make a wrapped loop (Basics, p. 12). Make two pearl units.

2 On an eye pin, string a flower bead and make a plain loop (Basics, p. 12).

3 On a head pin, string a rondelle and a leaf bar. Bend the wire into a right angle against the bar. Wrap it twice around your roundnose pliers and trim the excess.

4 Use the tip of your roundnose pliers to form a loop with a prong of a decorivet. Trim the remaining prong and file the edge if necessary.

5 Open a jump ring (Basics, p. 12) and attach the pendant and a pearl unit. Close the jump ring. Use another jump ring to attach a pearl unit and the loop of the decorivet.

6 Use a jump ring to attach one loop of the flower unit. Use another jump ring to attach the remaining loop and the hole of a bird charm.

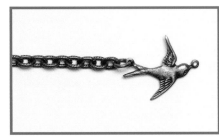

7 Cut a 15–17 in. (38–43 cm) piece of chain. Use a jump ring to attach one end to the remaining hole of the bird charm. Use a jump ring to attach the chain's other end and one hole of another bird charm.

8 Use a jump ring to attach the remaining hole of the bird charm and the loop of the leaf bar.

Hammering

• Protect your hearing: Place a sandbag, rubber block, or mat under your bench block.
• When imprinting letters, first practice on a piece of scrap metal to get a feel for how much pressure you need to apply.

Transferring images

• Use either preprinted water-slide transfers or create your own custom transfers.
• Keep in mind that the outer 4 mm of the canvas will be covered by the frame.

1 earrings • On a head pin, string a pearl and a rondelle. Make the first half of a wrapped loop (Basics, p. 12).

2 Attach the hole of a bird charm and complete the wraps. Open the loop of an eye pin (Basics, p. 12) and attach the remaining hole. Close the loop.

3 String a flower bead and make a plain loop (Basics, p. 12). Attach an earring wire and the dangle. Make a second earring.

Design alternative

For a quick pair of earrings, stamp two circles and attach beads and long earring wires.

Supplies

pendant
- 3-in. (7.6 cm) altered blank canvas
- 43 x 20 mm scrolled frame
- **2** ⅛-in. (3 mm) nail-head rivets
- bench block and rubber mat
- brass jeweler's hammer
- chasing hammer
- letter stamp set
- metal file
- metal two-hole punch or hole-punch pliers
- tin snips or cutting shears
- acrylic paint dabbers
- alcohol inks
- sharpie marker
- acrylic sealer (optional)
- digital rub-on or image transfer sheet (optional)

necklace 19 in. (48 cm)
- 10 mm glass flower bead
- 6 mm rondelle
- **2** 3 mm pearls
- 14.5 mm hobnail ring decorivet
- **2** 19 mm flying bird charms
- 1-in. (2.5 cm) eye pin
- **3** 1½-in. (3.8 cm) head pins
- **7** 4 mm jump rings
- 30 mm leaf creative bar
- 15–17 in. (38–43 cm) chain, 4–5 mm links
- chainnose and roundnose pliers
- diagonal wire cutters

earrings
- **2** 10 mm glass flower beads
- **2** 6 mm rondelles
- **2** 3 mm pearls
- **2** 19 mm flying bird charms
- **2** 1-in. (2.5 cm) 21-gauge eye pins
- **2** 1½-in. (3.8 cm) 24-gauge head pins
- pair of earring wires
- chainnose and roundnose pliers
- diagonal wire cutters

My personal
COLOR
quest

A faux verdigris patina is dominant in this set's color scheme

by Jane Konkel

For balanced color, use one shade in larger amounts.

I decided to launch my own personal color-mixing challenge. I'm very fond of Paloma Antigua's distressed metal charms, so I chose mint as my main color. Then I consulted a color wheel to help me choose the other three.

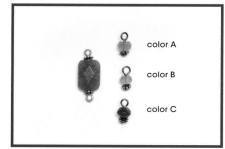

1 necklace • Trim the head from a head pin. Make a plain loop (Basics, p. 12). String a spacer, a rectangle bead, and a spacer. Make a plain loop. Make two rectangle bead units.

On a head pin, string a spacer and a color A rondelle. Make a plain loop. Make 17 to 25 color A units, three color B units, and three color C units.

2 Cut a 5½-in. (14 cm) and a 7-in. (18 cm) piece of leaf chain. Cut two 12–14-in. (30–36 cm) pieces of flat cable chain. Cut two nine-link pieces of flat-cable chain and three three-link pieces of leaf chain.

3 Open the loop (Basics, p. 12) of a color B unit and attach an end link of a nine-link chain. Close the loop. Attach a color C unit to the fifth link from the top.

4 Use a 4 mm jump ring to attach a 60 mm leaf pendant, the nine-link chain from step 3, and a three-link leaf chain. Close the jump ring. Make another embellished leaf, reversing the color of the bead units.

5 Use a 6 mm jump ring to attach a three-link leaf chain and a bird pendant.

Use a 4 mm jump ring to attach the bird-pendant dangle to the center link of the 7-in. (18 cm) leaf chain.

6 About 2 in. (5 cm) from each end of the 7-in. (18 cm) leaf chain, use a 4 mm jump ring to attach a leaf-pendant dangle.

7 Use 6 mm jump rings to attach the remaining charms to the 7-in. (18 cm) leaf chain. Attach a color B and a color C unit to the center link of the 5½-in. (14 cm) leaf chain.

8 Attach eight to 12 color A units to each chain as desired. Use a 4 mm jump ring to attach each loop of a rectangle bead unit, one end of each leaf chain, and each end of a 12–14-in. (30–36 cm) flat cable chain. Repeat on the other side.

9 Use a 4 mm jump ring to attach the center link of a cable chain and a lobster claw clasp.

On the center link of the other cable chain, attach three to six 6 mm jump rings. String a leaf (leftover from the cut chain), a color A unit, and a leaf before attaching the final jump ring.

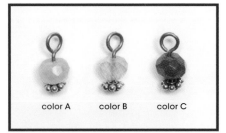

color A　color B　color C

1 bracelet • On a head pin, string a spacer and a color A rondelle. Make a plain loop (Basics, p. 12). Make 10 to 14 color A bead units, two color B units, and two color C units.

2 Cut a 3½–5-in. (8.9–13 cm) piece of leaf chain. Cut two 3¾–5¼-in. (9.5–13.3 cm) pieces of rolo chain and two 4–5½-in. (10–14 cm) pieces of flat-cable chain.

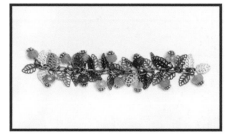

3 Open the loop (Basics, p. 12) of a color A bead unit and attach the center link of the leaf chain. On each side, skip a link and attach a color A unit. Skip a link and attach a color B and a color C unit. Attach a color A unit to every other link.

4 Use a 4 mm jump ring to attach each end of the beaded-leaf chain to the center hole of a leaf connector. Use 4 mm jump rings to attach each of the remaining chains and the corresponding hole of the leaf connector.

5 On each end, attach two 4 mm jump rings to the hole in the stem. On one end, use another 4 mm jump ring to attach a lobster claw clasp.

6 On the other end, attach three to six 6 mm jump rings. String a leaf (leftover from the cut chain), a color A unit, and a leaf before attaching the final jump ring.

Supplies

necklace 18 in. (46 cm)
- **7** 25–60 mm charms and pendants
- **2** 10 x 14 mm rectangle beads
- **23–31** 6 mm rondelles, **17–25** in dominant color, **6** in second and third colors
- **27–35** 4 mm flat spacers
- 15 in. (38 cm) leaf chain, 5 mm links
- 26–30 in. (66–76 cm) flat-cable chain, 3 mm links
- **25–33** 2-in. (5 cm) head pins
- **3–6** 6 mm jump rings
- **9** 4 mm jump rings
- lobster claw clasp
- chainnose and roundnose pliers
- diagonal wire cutters

bracelet
- **14–18** 6 mm rondelles, **10–14** in dominant color, **4** in second and third colors
- **14** 4 mm flat spacers
- **2** 30 mm five-to-one leaf connectors
- 4–5 in. (10–13 cm) leaf chain, 5 mm links
- 8–11 in. (20–28 cm) rolo chain, 4 mm links
- 8–11 in. (20–28 cm) flat-cable chain, 3 mm links
- **14–18** 2-in. (5 cm) head pins
- **4–6** 6 mm jump rings
- **15** 4 mm jump rings
- lobster claw clasp
- chainnose and roundnose pliers
- diagonal wire cutters

earrings
- **26** 6 mm rondelles, **10** in dominant color, **10** in second color, **6** in third color
- **14** 4 mm flat spacers
- **2** 50 mm crescent moon components
- **10** leaves, left over from leaf chain, 5 mm links
- 3 in. (7.6 cm) flat-cable chain, 3 mm links
- **4** 4 mm jump rings
- pair of earring wires
- **12** 2-in. (5 cm) head pins or eye pins (optional)
- chainnose and roundnose pliers
- diagonal wire cutters

66Life never seems to run out of challenges, so why not welcome them and learn something new?99 —Jane

1 earrings • Trim the head from a head pin and make a plain loop (Basics, p. 12). String: color B rondelle, spacer, color A rondelle, spacer, color B rondelle. Make a plain loop.

2 Open a loop (Basics, p. 12) of the bead unit and attach the second hole from the top of a crescent moon component. Close the loop. Attach the remaining loop to the hole on the other side.

3 Trim the head from a head pin and make a plain loop. String a color A, a flat spacer, and a color C. Make a plain loop. On one end, attach a leaf unit. Make five bead units as shown.

4 Attach the top loop of the center dangle to the bottom hole of the crescent moon. Attach the remaining dangles on each side of the center dangle.

5 Cut a 1½-in. (3.8 cm) piece of flat cable chain, making sure to cut an odd number of links. Attach the center link and the loop of an earring wire.

6 Use a jump ring to attach each end of the chain and a top loop of the crescent. Make a second earring.

SWITCHING style gears

Connect gears with jump rings in a mixed-metal bracelet

by Monica Han

I love pearls and crystals, but sometimes I think my jewelry designs are too safe and traditional. When I spotted these gears, my creative wheels started turning. Circles are just so versatile! This piece helped me think outside the box.

Supplies

bracelet
- ◆ **6–7** 25 mm (large) gears
- ◆ **6–7** 20 mm (small) gears
- ◆ **2** 22 mm open-center gears
- ◆ **60–80** 6–7 mm jump rings
- ◆ **2** toggle bars
- ◆ **2** pairs of pliers

earrings
- ◆ **2** 22 mm open-center gears
- ◆ **8** 6–7 mm jump rings
- ◆ pair of earring wires
- ◆ **2** pairs of pliers

Tim Holtz sprocket gears are available from select Michaels or timholtz.com

1 bracelet • Open a jump ring (Basics, p. 12). Attach a 25 mm (large) gear and a 20 mm (small) gear. Close the jump ring. Attach a second jump ring.

2 To make the first row, use pairs of jump rings to attach a total of six or seven large and small gears in an alternating pattern.

3 Make a second row of gears, attaching gears in the same finish but opposite size as in the first row.

4 Use two pairs of jump rings to attach the first gear in the first row to the first gear in the second row. Use two pairs of jump rings to attach each of the remaining gears in the two rows.

5 On one end of the first row, link three pairs of jump rings to attach an end gear and a toggle bar. Repeat on the same end of the second row.

6 On the other end, link one to three pairs of jump rings to attach an open-center gear (Adjusting the bracelet length). Repeat on the second row of gears.

1 earrings • Open a jump ring (Basics, p. 12). Attach an open-center gear. Close the jump ring. Attach a second jump ring.

2 Use a pair of jump rings to attach the previous pair of jump rings and the loop of an earring wire. Make a second earring.

Editor's Note

I liked these Tim Holtz tokens and made a simple, sentimental chain necklace with the initials of my newlywed friends.

Tips

- Tim Holtz gears are sold in packs of 12. Based on the assortment, to make a bracelet seven or more gears long, you'll need to buy three packs.
- For the earrings, make sure you use earring wires that have loops large enough to accommodate two jump rings.

Adjusting the bracelet length

You can vary the number of jump rings you use to attach the open-center gear. You can also attach an additional gear on each end. However, avoid removing jump rings from the toggle bar end — otherwise, you won't have enough room to maneuver the bar through the gear when clasping.

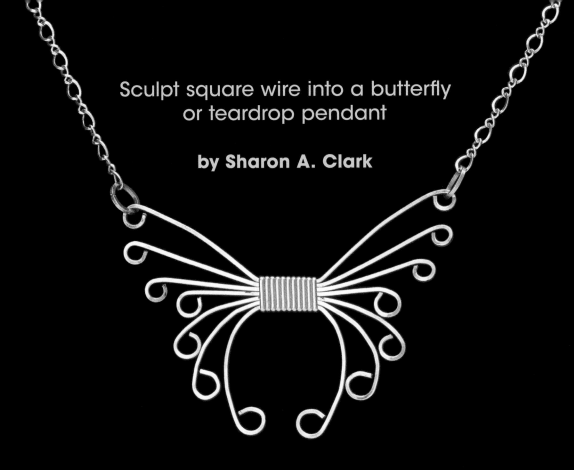

Sculpt square wire into a butterfly
or teardrop pendant

by Sharon A. Clark

Wire your way to
two beautiful
pendants

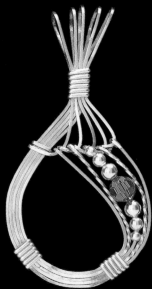

By learning a few techniques — bundling, wrapping,
twisting — you can transform wire into fantastic
pendants. The butterfly design went through several
prototypes before I was satisfied with it, and the
teardrop was inspired by a piece of vintage jewelry
that belonged to my mother. Mine doesn't look like
my mom's original piece, but it captures the same
spirit and I loved making it. If you're a beginner, don't
worry about perfection. Just enjoy the process of
playing with the square and half-round wire.

1 butterfly necklace • Cut seven 3½-in. (8.9 cm) pieces of square wire. Fold a twist tie around the wires near the center to make a temporary wrap, keeping the wires tight and parallel.

2 With a permanent marker, mark the center of the bundle. On each side, ¼ in. (6 mm) from the center, make a mark. Always mark the same side of the bundle — which will be the back side.

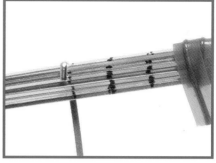

3 Cut a 6-in. (15 cm) piece of half-round wire. Holding the flat side toward you, bend your chainnose or flatnose pliers toward you to form a small hook. Place the hook on an outer mark of the bundle. Pull the wire around the bundle.

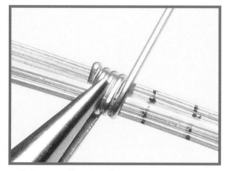

4 Grasp the half-round wrapping wire with chainnose pliers, and continue to pull the wire around the bundle, making tight, parallel wraps, until you've reached the outer mark. Trim the excess wrapping wire. Squeeze the ends of the wrapping wire down flat.

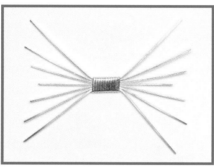

5 On one side of the wraps, splay the square wires. Mark and cut the wires as follows: the center wire, 9/16 in. (1.4 cm) from the end; the next two wires 3/8 in. (1 cm) from the end; the next two wires 3/16 in. (5 mm) from the end. Leave the two outer wires uncut. Repeat on the other side of the wraps.

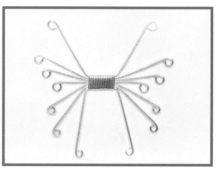

6 On each side of the wraps: Using roundnose pliers, make a loop on an outer wire. Repeat on the next three wires, making each loop face the same direction as the first. Make loops on the remaining wires. If desired, make the bottom three loops slightly larger than the top four loops.

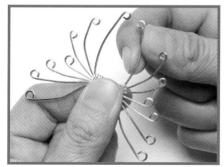

7 Using your fingers, pull the bottom two wires toward each other. Curve the remaining wires as desired.

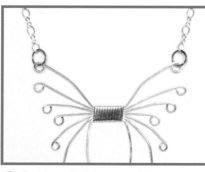

8 Cut two 7–9-in. (18–23 cm) pieces of chain. Open a 7 mm jump ring (Basics, p. 12). Attach one of the top loops of the pendant and a chain. Close the jump ring. Repeat on the other side of the pendant.

9 Check the fit, and trim chain if necessary. On one end, use a jump ring to attach a lobster claw clasp. Repeat on the other end, substituting a soldered jump ring for the clasp.

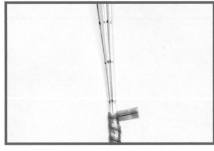

1 teardrop pendant • Cut five 8-in. (20 cm) pieces of square wire. Fold a twist tie around the wires near the center to make a temporary wrap, keeping the wires tight and parallel. Mark the bundle 2½ in. (6.4 cm) from one end. On each side, ⅝ in. (1.6 cm) from the first mark, make a mark.

2 Center the 2½-in. (6.4 cm) mark on a pencil and curve the bundle around it (with the marks on the outside).

3 Just below the ⅝-in. (1.6 cm) marks, fold a twist tie around all the wires. Cut a 2½-in. (6.4 cm) piece of half-round wire. Holding the flat side toward you, bend your chainnose or flatnose pliers toward you to form a small hook. With the longer wires facing you, place the hook on the ⅝-in. (1.6 cm) mark. Pull the wire around the bundle.

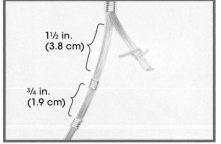

4 Grasping the wrapping wire with chainnose pliers, continue to pull the wire around the bundle six times. Trim the excess wrapping wire and squeeze the ends of the wrapping wire down flat.

5 Splay the loops above the wraps. Pull the shorter wires to the right and the longer wires to the left.

6 Mark the longer wires 1½ in. (3.8 cm) from the edge of the wraps. Cut a 2½-in. (6.4 cm) piece of half-round wire. Starting from the unmarked side of the wires, make five wraps. Trim the excess wire. With a second piece of wire, make another set of five wraps ¾ in. (1.9 cm) from the edge of the wraps you just made.

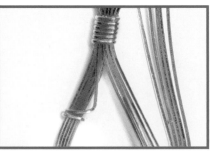

7 With your fingers, curve the bundled wires into a drop shape. The bottom of the drop will be the space between the two sets of wraps you just made.

8 Bend the first short wire down and to the left. Wrap the wire around the bundle twice and trim the excess.

9 Bend the next wire toward the first. Make a small loop around the first wire and trim the excess. Attach each of the remaining short wires to the previous one in the same way.

10 Bring the first long wire across the pendant. Go through the first wire from step 9 and make a loop. Trim the excess wire.

11 Grasp the next wire with chainnose pliers. Rotate the pliers to twist the wire. Bring the wire across the pendant and through the next wire from step 9. Make a loop and trim the excess wire.

12 On the next wire, string two or three round spacers in increasing order of size, a round crystal, and two or three round spacers in decreasing order of size. Attach the wire to the next wire from step 9.

13 Twist and attach the next wire. Attach the last wire as shown. Use your fingers to adjust the drop shape as necessary.

Design alternative

Use the techniques you've learned — bundling and splaying the wire and making loops — to create a feather pendant.

66 Have fun. Relax. There is never a mistake; you just make it part of your design. A broken wire can be curled, looped, or tucked in. **99** —Sharon

Supplies

butterfly necklace
18 in. (46 cm)
- 14–18 in. (36–46 cm) chain, 3–4 mm links
- 25 in. (64 cm) 20-gauge half-hard square wire
- 6 in. (15 cm) 18-gauge half-hard, half-round wire
- twist ties
- **2** 7 mm jump rings
- **2** 4 mm jump rings
- lobster claw clasp and soldered jump ring
- chainnose or flatnose pliers
- roundnose pliers
- diagonal wire cutters
- permanent marker

teardrop pendant
- 6 mm round crystal
- **2** 4 mm round spacers
- **2** 3 mm round spacers
- 40 in. (1 m) 21-gauge half-hard square wire
- 8 in. (20 cm) 18-gauge half-hard, half-round wire
- twist ties
- chainnose or flatnose pliers
- roundnose pliers
- diagonal wire cutters
- pencil
- permanent marker
- **2** 2 mm round spacers (optional)

Tip

The price of sterling wire fluctuates, so check a few sources before you buy. Also, make sure you're comparing prices for the same quantities. Some suppliers sell by the foot; some, by the ounce.

String a vintage
look that captures
today's fashion

by Angela Bannatyne

Chances
are you
already
have
plenty of
coordinated
beads in
your stash.

Tip

Arrange the bead
units on a bead board
to balance the colors
and sizes before
attaching them
to the chain.

Time-traveling

I love this piece because it's relevant and current but at the same time has a wonderful vintage feel. The multicolored beads make it very versatile. It's also a great way to use up your bead stash.

Supplies

necklace 39 in. (99 cm)
- 22 mm oval faceted glass bead
- **3** 14 mm (large) pearls
- **5** 12 mm (small) pearls
- **4** 12 mm crystal saucers
- **34** 8 mm fire-polished crystals
- **5** 7 mm textured round metal beads
- **5** 8º seed beads
- **5** 4 mm round spacers
- **3** 4 mm flat spacers
- **5** 8 mm bead caps
- 10 in. (25 cm) ¼-in. (6 mm) ribbon
- 73–76 in. (1.8–1.9 m) chain, 6–10 mm links
- **52** 2-in. (5 cm) head pins
- **2** 16 mm decorative jump rings
- 10 mm jump ring
- chainnose and roundnose pliers
- diagonal wire cutters
- scissors

earrings
- **2** 8 mm fire-polished crystals
- **4** 4 mm round spacers
- **2** chain links left over from necklace
- **2** 2-in. (5 cm) head pins
- **2** 2-in. (5 cm) eye pins
- pair of earring wires
- chainnose and roundnose pliers
- diagonal wire cutters

1 necklace • On a head pin, string a 12 mm pearl, a bead cap, and a round spacer. Make the first half of a wrapped loop (Basics, p. 12). Make five 12 mm (small) pearl units.

On a head pin, string a fire-polished crystal or saucer bead. Make a plain loop (Basics, p. 12). Make 34 fire-polished units and four saucer units.

On a head pin, string an 8º seed bead and a 7 mm metal bead. Make five metal-bead units.

On a head pin, string a flat spacer and a 14 mm pearl. Make a plain loop. Make three 14 mm (large) pearl units.

2 Cut a 14-in. (36 cm) piece of chain. Open the loop of a large-pearl unit (Basics, p. 12) and attach the center link. Close the loop. On each side, within 4 in. (10 cm) of the center unit, attach three large- and three small-pearl units.

66 I am inspired by fashion, so my style changes based on current trends. **99** —Angela

3 Attach a metal-bead unit and seven to 10 fire-polished or saucer units between the pearl units.

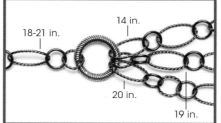

4 Cut three pieces of chain: 18–21 in. (46–53 cm), 19 in. (48 cm), and 20 in. (51 cm). Open a 16 mm decorative jump ring (Basics, p. 12) and attach an end link of the 18–21-in. 20-in., 19-in., and 14-in. chains, in that order. Close the jump ring. Repeat on the other ends of the chains.

trendsetter

Design alternative

Changing the components can create an endless number of styles.

5 On a head pin, string a 22 mm bead. Make the first half of a wrapped loop. Cut a 2-in. (5 cm) piece of chain. Attach the bead unit and complete the wraps.

6 Attach two fire-polished units to the dangle. Use a 10 mm jump ring to attach a small-pearl unit, the dangle, a metal-bead unit, and the 16 mm jump ring.

7 Cut a 10-in. (25 cm) piece of ribbon. Tie a bow around a 16 mm jump ring.

1 earrings •
On an eye pin, string two round spacers. Make a plain loop (Basics, p. 12).

2 Following necklace step 1, make a fire-polished unit. Open the loops of the eye-pin unit (Basics, p, 12). Attach the bead unit to one loop and a chain link to the other. Close the loops.

3 Open the loop of an earring wire. Attach the dangle and close the loop. Make a second earring.

Pressed for time

Mix wristwatches and metal arrows for a pair of earrings lickety-split

By Jane Konkel

Reclaimed mechanical watch movements and brass game spinners will give you steampunk style in no time.

1 Use a metal hole punch to punch a hole at the center of the top circle of a game spinner.

2 Use two-part epoxy to glue a mechanical watch movement to the spinner. Allow to dry.

Supplies

- ◆ **2** 57 mm game spinners
- ◆ **2** 18 mm mechanical watch movements
- ◆ **2** 7 mm jump rings
- ◆ pair of earring wires
- ◆ **2** pairs of pliers
- ◆ metal hole punch
- ◆ two-part epoxy
- ◆ Liquid Paper (optional)

Tim Holtz Ideology game spinners from Rings & Things, rings-things.com.

3 Open a jump ring (Basics, p. 12). Attach the dangle and the loop of an earring wire. Close the jump ring. Make a second earring.

Tip

To punch centered holes in the game spinners, position the center circle of one drilled spinner over the top circle of the other spinner. Use Liquid Paper to mark the hole at the center.

Wire-wrap a web

Celebrate Halloween year round with cute and devilish earrings

By Criss Hunt

The first time I made a lampworked bead, I knew what I wanted to do for the rest of my life. I enjoy whatever is bright, fun, and goofy, so the whimsical style stuck. Recently, I discovered wire wrapping and it adds a whole new dimension to my work!

A parade of Halloween beads makes for a no-trick, all-treat bracelet.

Let Criss' other earring creations inspire your next wirework project.

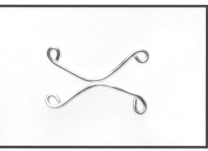

1 To make a radial wire: Cut a 2-in. (5 cm) piece of 18-gauge wire. Using roundnose pliers, make a small loop at one end. String a spider bead. At the other end, make a small loop in the opposite direction as the first loop.

2 Repeat step 1 to make two more radial wires without spider beads. Using a mandrel or barrel of a pen, curve the wires gently at their center. Position them as shown.

3 Cut a 25-in. (64 cm) piece of 24- or 26-gauge wire. Wrap one end around the center of the curved radial wires three or four times.

Supplies

- **2** 8–10 mm spider beads
- 12 in. (30 cm) 18-gauge half-hard wire
- 50 in. (1.3 m) 24- or 26-gauge half-hard wire
- pair of earring wires
- chainnose and roundnose pliers
- diagonal wire cutters
- mandrel or pen

All beads shown from Criss Hunt, handmadebeads.com.

4 Center the radial wire from step 1 on top of the wraps. Randomly wrap the 24- or 26-gauge wire around all three radial wires until secure. Pinch together the wraps to create a dense "hub" at the center of the web.

5 With the remaining 24- or 26-gauge wire, wrap once around the nearest radial wire, then wrap around an adjacent radial wire. Repeat. When you reach the radial wire with the spider, wrap above the bead.

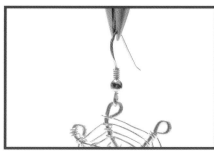

Tip

Using 26-gauge wire to wrap around the radial wires creates a denser web than 24-gauge wire. Colored wire offers another fun option.

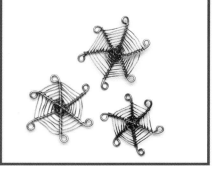

6 Continue wrapping around the radial wires, but each time you reach the spider bead, wrap below it. When your wraps reach the radial wires' loops, wrap several times around a radial wire near the loop. Trim the excess wire and tuck the end.

7 Open the loop of an earring wire (Basics, p. 12). Attach the loop of a radial wire and close the loop. Make a second earring.

Random acts of style

Say goodbye to methodical and hello to messy

by Jenny Van

Sometimes order is overrated. For this design, randomly attach a variety of beads to three pieces of chain, then connect the chains at irregular intervals. Go ahead, throw caution to the wind — at least for the time it takes to make this bracelet.

1 bracelet • On a head pin, string a bead. Make the first half of a wrapped loop (Basics, p. 12). On a head pin, string a spacer and a bead. Make the first half of a wrapped loop. Make 12 to 16 bead units and six to eight spacer-and-bead units.

2 On a head pin, string a top-drilled crystal. Make a right-angle bend in back of the crystal. Make the first half of a wrapped loop. Make two top-drilled units.

3 Open a jump ring (Basics, p. 12) and attach one loop of a clasp. Close the jump ring. Attach a jump ring to each loop on both halves of the clasp.

4 Cut three 6–8-in. (15–20 cm) pieces of chain. Use a jump ring to attach a chain and a jump ring on one half of the clasp. Repeat with the remaining chains.

5 Attach a top-drilled unit to a link of chain and complete the wraps. Attach eight to 10 bead units to the chain, completing the wraps as you go.

6 Attach the remaining bead units to the other chains.

7 Attach a jump ring to a link of the first chain. Use another jump ring to attach the first jump ring to a link of the second chain. Use six pairs of jump rings to attach the first and second chains and six pairs of jump rings to attach the second and third chains.

8 Use jump rings to attach the end link of each chain and the jump rings on the other half of the clasp.

Supplies

bracelet
- **18–24** 6–15 mm beads and pearls in a variety of shapes
- **2** 13 mm top-drilled crystals
- **6–8** 2 mm round spacers
- 18–24 in. (46–61 cm) chain, 3–4 mm links
- **20–26** 2-in. (5 cm) head pins
- **36** 4 mm jump rings
- three-strand box clasp
- chainnose and roundnose pliers
- diagonal wire cutters

earrings
- **16** 10 mm beads
- **16** 1½-in. (3.8 cm) head pins
- **2** 4 mm jump rings
- pair of earring wires
- chainnose and roundnose pliers
- diagonal wire cutters

1 earrings • On a head pin, string a bead. Make a plain loop (Basics, p. 12). Make eight bead units.

2 Open a jump ring (Basics, p. 12). Attach six bead units and the loop of an earring wire. Close the jump ring.

3 Open the loop of a bead unit (Basics, p. 12) and attach the loop of the earring wire. Close the loop. Attach a second bead unit to the earring wire's loop. Make a second earring.

Tip

To ensure the clasp is oriented correctly, close the clasp before attaching the chains in step 8.

Design alternative

In this version, I substituted heart charms for the top-drilled crystals.

"I like my bracelets because they're stylish and affordable to make." –Jenny

Media

Get inspired by
spring's prettiest palette

Let a mix of colors guide a playful design

by Naomi Fujimoto

Lightweight resin chain forms a casual backdrop for bright crystals and Lucite.

This piece is a bright combination of warm and cool tones. I started with Lucite beads in coral, mint, turquoise, ocean blue, and honeysuckle, and added crystals and a touch of gold to complete the mix. Though you can easily substitute gold chain (or gunmetal, if you prefer an edgier look), this resin chain was a perfect match.

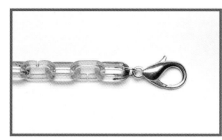

1 necklace • On a head pin, string a flat spacer and a Lucite bead. Using the largest part of your roundnose pliers, make a plain loop (Basics, p. 12). Repeat to make a crystal unit and a metal-bead unit, omitting the spacer. Make 60 to 84 bead units, plus one for step 6.

2 Decide how long you want your necklace to be and cut a piece of chain to that length. Open the loop of a bead unit (Basics, p. 12). Attach the center link and close the loop. Attach three more bead units to the center link.

3 On each side, attach four bead units to each link. Repeat the pattern of 12 beads (I attached two repeats on each side of the center pattern).

4 Check the fit, and remove chain if necessary. On one end, open a jump ring (Basics, p. 12). Attach a lobster claw clasp and close the jump ring. Repeat on the other end, substituting a soldered jump ring for the clasp.

5 Cut a 3-in. (7.6 cm) piece of chain. Use a jump ring to attach the short chain and the soldered jump ring.

6 Attach a bead unit to the end link of the extender.

Tip
Don't use diagonal wire cutters to trim resin chain. Instead, gently open the links with two pairs of pliers.

"After a season of black and grey, I'm ready for some color!" —Naomi

Design alternative

For a casual necklace that showcases individual beads, attach one bead unit to every other chain link. Add a pair of simple drop earrings.

Tip

String spacers to act as stoppers for the Lucite beads, which have large holes and will otherwise slip off the head pins. Keep the crystals unembellished, but if you like a more elegant or consistent style, use spacers on all of the bead units.

1 bracelet • Cut a piece of beading wire (Basics, p. 13). String beads and flat spacers as desired until the strand is within 1 in. (2.5 cm) of the finished length.

2 On each end, add half of a toggle clasp (Basics, p. 13).

3 Follow step 1 of the necklace instructions to make a bead unit. Open the loop (Basics, p. 12) and attach the loop half of the clasp. Close the loop.

Supplies

necklace 16 in. (41 cm)
- **29–40** 7–14 mm Lucite beads
- **27–40** 8–10 mm crystals
- **5–8** 8–10 mm metal beads
- **29–88** 3–5 mm flat spacers
- 18–23 in. (46–58 cm) resin chain, 14 mm links
- **61–88** 1½-in. (3.8 cm) head pins
- **3** 6–7 mm jump rings
- large lobster claw clasp and soldered jump ring
- chainnose and roundnose pliers
- diagonal wire cutters

bracelet
- **9–11** 7–14 mm Lucite beads
- **5–7** 8–10 mm crystals
- **1–2** 8–10 mm metal beads
- **14–19** 3–5 mm flat spacers
- **2** 3–4 mm spacers
- flexible beading wire, .014 or .015
- 1½-in. (3.8 cm) head pin
- **2** crimp beads
- **2** Wire Guardians
- toggle clasp
- chainnose and roundnose pliers
- diagonal wire cutters
- crimping pliers (optional)

earrings
- **4** 7–14 mm Lucite beads
- **2** 8–10 mm crystals
- **4–6** 3–5 mm flat spacers
- **2** links resin chain, 14 mm links
- **6** 1½-in. (3.8 cm) head pins
- **2** 6–7 mm jump rings
- pair of earring wires
- chainnose and roundnose pliers
- diagonal wire cutters

1 earrings • Follow step 1 of the necklace instructions to make three bead units.

2 Open the loop of a bead unit (Basics, p. 12). Attach a chain link and close the loop.

3 Open a jump ring (Basics, p. 12). Attach a bead unit, the link, a bead unit, and the loop of an earring wire. Close the jump ring. Make a second earring.

Playing with color

- In addition to using different colors, I wanted to combine glossy, opalescent, and transparent beads. So I bought a variety of Lucite strands and laid them out next to Pantone's Fashion Color Report. (Visit pantone.com and search "fashion color report" to download your own copy.)

- If you're unsure of how to create a palette, mixes of Lucite beads can be a great starting point

- I used Swarovski Elements crystals in Indian pink, Provence lavender, sunflower, and Capri blue. I also included silk and smoked topaz as neutrals to ground the palette and make it less rainbow-y. If you want to include more crystals, consider rose, turquoise, Pacific opal, aquamarine champagne, mint alabaster, or black diamond.

Unwrap a double- or triple-wrap bracelet and attach a pendant to make a necklace.

double-wrap bracelet

When I was gathering the supplies to make these Chan Luu-style leather bracelets, Dawn Sklare from Chelsea's Beads offered me a few pointers. She told me large-hole beads are a must, and to use an extra strand of beads and two cards of silk cord for a triple-wrap bracelet. By tying the ends of the silk cord together and anchoring the knot under the first bead, you can make an extra-long bracelet that can also serve as a necklace.

Leather wrap

Simplicity and charm combine in a wearable, wraparound, unisex bracelet

by Jane Konkel

1 single-wrap bracelet • Cut a piece of leather cord (Cutting cord, p. 118). Center a button on the cord. With both ends, tie an overhand knot (Basics, p. 12) next to the button.

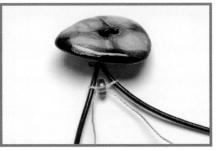

2 String a twisted-wire needle on the end of a silk cord without the attached needle. Center a bead on the silk cord. Center the strung bead between the leather cords near the button. Bring each end of the silk cord around the leather cords and up through the middle. To anchor the bead, string each end of the silk cord through the bead in opposite directions.

triple-wrap
bracelet

single-wrap
bracelet

double-
wrap
bracelet

bracelet

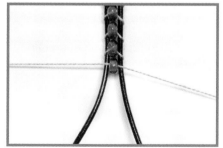

3 Bring each end of the silk cord around the leather cords and up through the middle again. String the silk cord in opposite directions through the next bead, Pull the ends of the silk cord to tighten it.

4 Continue stringing beads as in step 3 until your bracelet is within 3 in. (7.6 cm) of the finished length. String the silk cord through the last bead again, and tie two or three surgeon's knots (Basics, p. 12) to anchor the bead. Apply glue to the knots and trim the excess silk cord. The knot may or may not slip inside the last bead.

5 With both ends of the leather cord, tie an overhand knot next to the last bead. Tie another overhand knot to form a loop to accommodate the button. Trim the excess leather.

Supplies

- 15–30 mm button with shank
- **1–2** 16-in. (41 cm) strands 4–6 mm large-hole beads
- **1–2** cards silk beading cord with attached needle, size 2
- 24–52 in. (.61–1.3 m) 2–4 mm round leather cord
- twisted-wire beading needle
- diagonal wire cutters
- G-S Hypo Cement

Tip

If the shank of the button is too small to accommodate the leather cord, attach two 5–6 mm jump rings to the shank and center the jump rings on the cord.

double-wrap bracelet or choker •
Follow step 1 of the single-wrap bracelet.

With an overhand knot (Basics, p. 12), tie together the non-needle ends of two silk cords. Apply glue to the knot. Trim the excess silk cord. Center a bead over the knot.

Anchor the bead as in step 2 of the single-wrap bracelet. Follow steps 3 through 5 of the single-wrap bracelet.

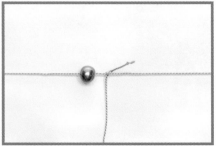

triple-wrap bracelet • Follow step 1 of the single-wrap bracelet.

With an overhand knot (Basics, p. 12), tie together the non-needle ends of two silk cords. Trim the excess silk cord. Apply glue to the knot. Center a bead over the knot.

Anchor the bead as in step 2 of the single-wrap bracelet. Follow steps 3 through 5 of the single-wrap bracelet.

Cutting cord

- For a single-wrap bracelet, cut a 24-in. (61 cm) piece of leather cord.
- For a double-wrap bracelet, cut a 40-in. (1 m) piece.
- For a triple-wrap bracelet, cut a 52-in. (1.3 m) piece.

Supply notes

- Pendant, brass spacers, and copper spacers from Hands of the Hills, hohbead.com.
- Purple glass rondelles from Rings & Things, rings-things.com.
- Green ceramic rectangle beads from Clay River Designs, clayriverdesigns.com.
- Large-hole pearls from Chelsea's Beads, chelseasbeads.com.
- Mermaid button from Green Girl Studios, greengirlstudios.com.
- Leather cord from Leather Cord USA, leathercordusa.com.
- Tumbled glass toggle button from Glass Garden Beads, glassgardenbeads.com.

Stylish
through & through

A bead-through button component makes this multistrand bracelet a breeze

by Dee Perry

When it comes to choosing beads to go with this focal piece, there's really no wrong choice; the multiple colors in the inset offer many options. I chose beads in an analogous color family that echoed the shimmery finish.

You can easily adjust this design to make a choker.

Supplies

bracelet
- Bead-Thru button component
- **36–40** 12 mm briolettes
- **10–12** 12 mm faceted glass nuggets
- **60–70** 5–8 mm assorted potato and keshi pearls
- 1 g E beads
- 1 g 11º seed beads
- flexible beading wire, .014 or .015
- **10** crimp beads

- **10** crimp covers (optional) five-strand slide clasp
- chainnose or crimping pliers
- diagonal wire cutters

earrings
- **2** 12 mm polygon crystals
- **8** 5 mm potato pearls
- 5 in. (13 cm) 22-gauge wire
- **8** 1½-in. (3.8 cm) head pins
- pair of earring wires

- chainnose and roundnose pliers
- diagonal wire cutters

Bead-Thru button component from Claspon-Claspoff, claspon-claspoff.com.

1 bracelet • Cut five 12-in. (30 cm) pieces of beading wire. On one wire, string 3–4 in. (7.6–10 cm) of alternating E beads and polygon crystals. On each of the remaining four wires, string 3–4 in. (7.6–10 cm) of potato pearls, keshi pearls, E beads, and briolettes, varying the pattern on each wire.

2 String all five strands through one side of the button component. On each wire, string enough 11º seed beads to fill the component. String the other side of the button component. Repeat the patterns from step 1.

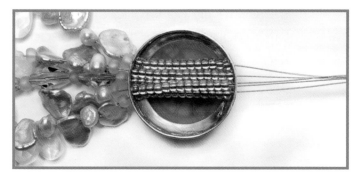

3 On each end of each wire, string a crimp bead and a loop of a slide clasp. Check the fit, and add or remove beads if necessary. Go back through the beads just strung and tighten the wires. Crimp the crimp beads (Basics, p. 12) and trim the excess wire.

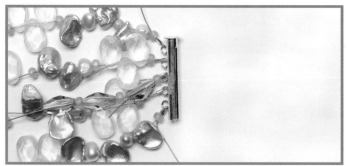

"The Bead-Thru component was inspired by vintage buttons." —Dee

1 earrings • Cut a 2½-in. (6.4 cm) piece of wire. Make a wrapped loop (Basics, p. 12). String a polygon crystal and make a wrapped loop.

2 On a head pin, string a potato pearl. Make the first half of a wrapped loop. Make four pearl units.

3 Attach the pearl units to one loop of the polygon unit and complete the wraps. Open the loop of an earring wire (Basics p. 12). Attach the dangle and close the loop. Make a second earring.

Petals & pastels

An easy bracelet is a breath of fresh air

by Naomi Fujimoto

It's always fun to string simple dangles and big beads.
A preppy mix of pink, white, and green in this sampler
made this design a breeze!

Supplies

- **5-6** 15–23 mm Lucite leaf beads
- **30–40** 6–17 mm Lucite flower beads
- **11–14** 12 mm round faceted glass beads or crystals
- **20–30** 3 mm bicone crystals
- 1 g 11º seed beads
- **2** 3–4 mm round spacers
- flexible beading wire, .018 or .019
- 1½ in. (3.8 cm) chain, 10–15 mm links
- **16–19** 1½-in. (3.8 cm) head pins
- **2** crimp beads
- lobster claw clasp
- chainnose and roundnose pliers
- diagonal wire cutters

1 On a head pin, string a bicone crystal and one or two flowers. (If the second flower has a large hole, string another bicone after it.) Make a wrapped loop (Basics, p. 12). Make 15 to 21 flower units.

2 Open a jump ring (Basics p. 12). Attach a leaf and close the jump ring. Make five or six leaf units.

3 Cut a piece of beading wire (Basics, p. 13). String: 12 mm round bead, 11º seed bead, three flower units, 12 mm, leaf unit, 11º. Repeat until the strand is within 1 in. (2.5 cm) of the finished length. End with a 12 mm.

4 On one end, add a clasp (Basics, p. 13). Repeat on the other end, substituting a 1½-in. (3.8 cm) chain for the clasp.

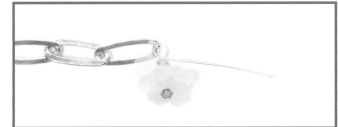

5 On a head pin, string a bicone, one or two flowers, and a bicone. Make the first half of a wrapped loop. Attach the end of the chain and complete the wraps.

Design alternative

If you fancy foliage, make a pair of earrings with different green leaf beads.

Beaded
BRAIDS

Braid assorted textures in a colorful cuff

by Kimberly Wayne

This cuff is a mix of calm and crazy: I started with a complementary color palette — purple and green — then found a neutral balancing shade so the bracelet would be less busy. I braided everything from teensy seed beads to faceted pyrite nuggets and sparkling crystals. Invent your own combination and see what takes shape!

1 bracelet · Cut 10 16–19-in. (41–48 cm) pieces of beading wire. On one wire, string a crimp bead and the center loop of a slide clasp (Finishing, p. 126). Go back through the crimp bead and tighten the wire. Crimp the crimp bead (Basics, p. 12) and trim the excess wire. Attach two more wires to the same loop of the clasp.

2 On one wire, string 9–12 in. (23–30 cm) of cube beads or 11º seed beads.

On the second wire, string three 4 mm or four 3 mm bicone crystals, then a round crystal. Repeat until the strand is the same length as the first.

On the third wire, string a 6 mm and a 4 mm bicone crystal. Repeat until the strand is the same length as the first. Tape the ends of each strand as you go.

3 Attach three pieces of beading wire to an outer loop of the clasp half. On each wire, string 9–12 in. (23–30 cm) of beads: a gemstone strand, a pearl strand, and a 3 mm bicone strand. Tape the ends of each strand as you go.

4 Attach four pieces of beading wire to the remaining loop of the clasp half. On each wire, string 9–12 in. (23–30 cm) of beads: a pyrite strand, an 8º seed bead strand, and two 13º or 15º seed bead strands. Tape the ends of each strand as you go.

Supplies

bracelet

- 16-in. (41 cm) strand 5–6 mm pyrite nuggets
- 16-in. (41 cm) strand 4 mm pearls
- 16-in. (41 cm) strand 3–4 mm gemstones
- **15–19** 6 mm round crystals
- **25–30** 6 mm bicone crystals
- **24–75** 4 mm bicone crystals
- **100–180** 3 mm bicone crystals
- 2–3 g 8º seed beads
- 2 g 1.5 mm cube beads or 11º hex-cut seed beads
- 1–2 g 13º or 15º seed beads
- flexible beading wire, .014 or .015
- **20** crimp beads
- three-strand slide clasp
- chainnose or crimping pliers
- diagonal wire cutters
- foam board
- T-pin

earrings

- **2** 6 mm round crystals
- **2** 4 mm bicone crystals
- **2** 3 mm bicone crystals
- **6** 1½-in. (3.8 cm) head pins
- 4 in. (10 cm) cable chain, 2–3 mm links
- pair of earring posts with ear nuts
- chainnose and roundnose pliers
- diagonal wire cutters

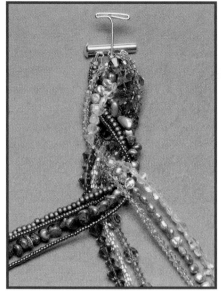

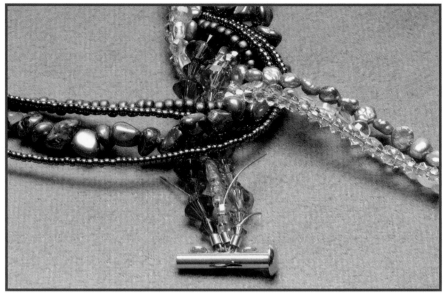

5 Use a T-pin to secure the clasp to a foam board. Keeping each set of strands flat, braid the sets until the bracelet is the desired length.

6 On each end of the three center strands, string a crimp bead and the corresponding loop of the other half of the clasp. Check the fit and add or remove beads if necessary. Go back through the beads just strung and tighten the wire. Crimp the crimp bead and trim the excess wire. Attach the remaining sets of strands and the corresponding loop of the clasp.

❝I found a braided string bracelet I got when I was young. I thought it would be an awesome update with leftover crystals and gemstones.❞ –Kimberly

Flexible beading wire

If you string .010 beading wire, it's easier to finish the seed bead strands, but I used .014 because it holds up better to frequent wire tightening.

Finishing

- Attach three wires to the center loop of the clasp before attaching the outer wires (otherwise it will be difficult to crimp).
- It's easier to make flattened crimps than folded crimps (Basics, p. 12).
- If desired, on each end of the wire, string a seed bead or a 3 mm bicone before stringing the crimp bead so you'll have a place to tuck the trimmed wire after crimping.

1 earrings • On a head pin, string a crystal. Make a plain loop (Basics, p. 12). Make three crystal units.

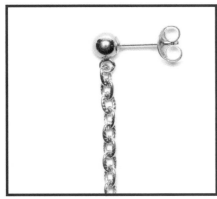

2 Open the loop of an earring post (Basics, p. 12). Attach the end link of a chain (Earring tip, below) and close the loop.

3 Near the loop of the post, tie an overhand knot (Basics, p. 12) with the chain. Do not trim the excess chain.

4 Open the loop of the round-crystal unit (Basics, p. 12). Attach a link of chain just below the knot and close the loop. Trim the excess chain. Attach the 4 mm bicone unit to the same link as the round unit. Attach the 3 mm bicone unit to another link. Make a second earring.

Tip

You'll need only about an inch of chain per earring, but it's easier to start with a longer piece and knot it, attach the bead units, and then trim the excess chain. It's also easier to make the first earring and then a second to match (rather than first cutting the two pieces of chain).

All the WOW without the WEAVE

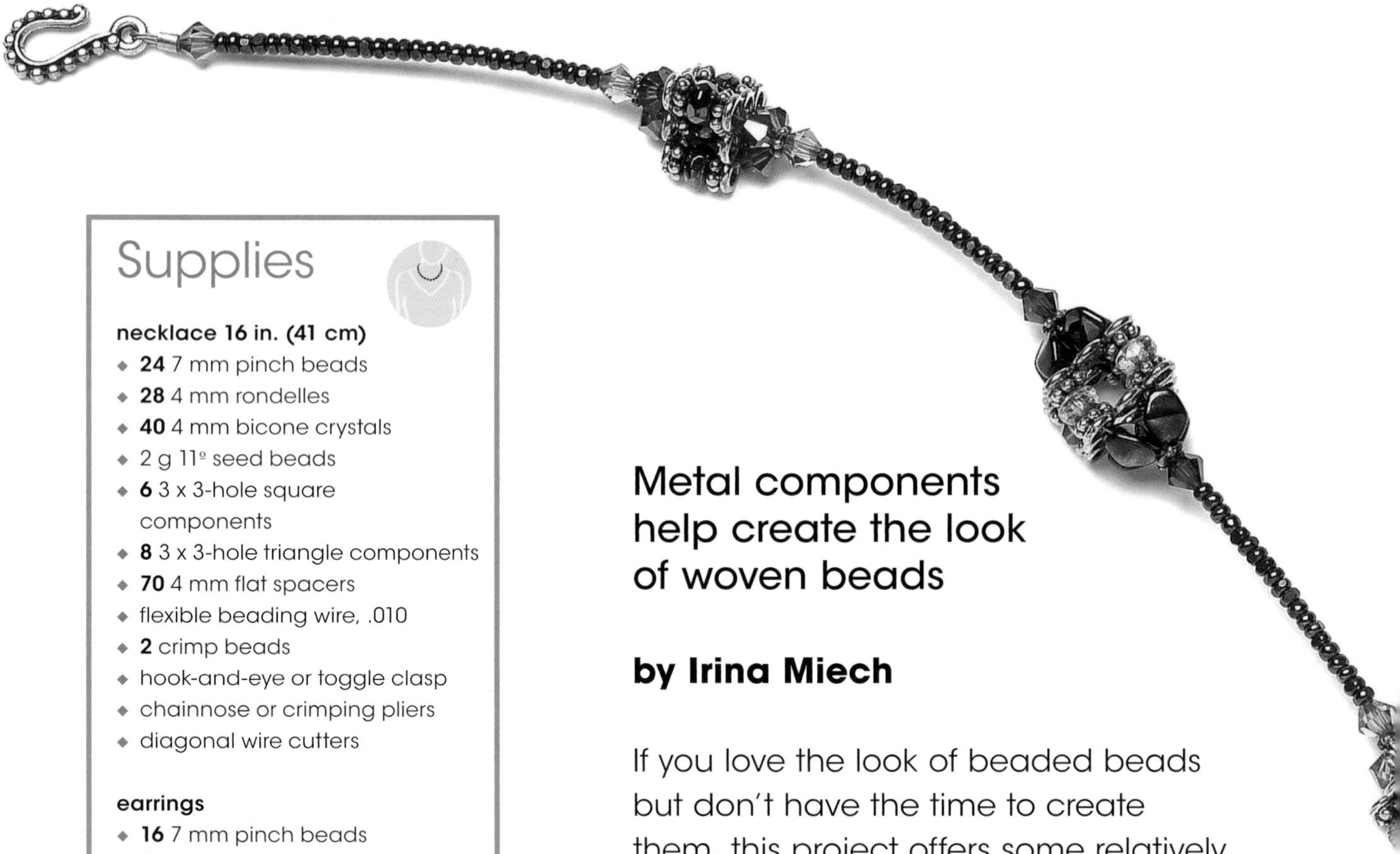

Supplies

necklace 16 in. (41 cm)
- **24** 7 mm pinch beads
- **28** 4 mm rondelles
- **40** 4 mm bicone crystals
- 2 g 11º seed beads
- **6** 3 x 3-hole square components
- **8** 3 x 3-hole triangle components
- **70** 4 mm flat spacers
- flexible beading wire, .010
- **2** crimp beads
- hook-and-eye or toggle clasp
- chainnose or crimping pliers
- diagonal wire cutters

earrings
- **16** 7 mm pinch beads
- **8** 4 mm rondelles
- **4** 4 mm bicone crystals
- **2** 11º seed beads
- **2** 3 x 3-hole square components
- **20** 4 mm flat spacers
- 18 in. (46 cm) 30-gauge dead-soft wire
- pair of earring wires
- chainnose and roundnose pliers
- diagonal wire cutters

Metal components help create the look of woven beads

by Irina Miech

If you love the look of beaded beads but don't have the time to create them, this project offers some relatively immediate gratification. As a bonus, you probably have most of the materials needed in your stash right now. The key to this three-dimensional construction are the square and triangular components that support the beads.

Beaded beads

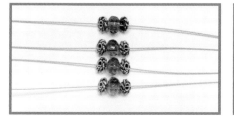

1 square bead • Cut four 25-in. (64 cm) pieces of beading wire. On each wire, center a flat spacer, a rondelle, and a flat spacer.

2 On each end of each wire, string a corner hole of a square component.

3 On each end of each wire, string a pinch bead. On each side, over all four wires, string a flat spacer and a bicone crystal. For subsequent square beads, string the beads from end to end instead of starting from the center.

66 Depending on the colors you use, this necklace can be a formal or fun accessory. **99** —Irina

4 On each side, make a square bead. String 18 to 20 11ºs. Make a triangle bead. String 11ºs until the strand is within 1 in. (2.5 cm) of the finished length. Check the fit and add or remove 11ºs if necessary.

5 On each side, over all four wires, string a bicone and add a clasp (Basics, p. 12).

3 On each side, make a triangle bead (p. 130). Over all four wires, string 18 to 20 11ºs.

1 necklace • Make a square bead (Beaded beads, above).

2 On each side, over all four wires, string 18 to 20 11º seed beads.

1 triangle bead • Over all four wires, string a bicone crystal and a flat spacer.

2 On each of three wires, string a bicone and the corner hole of a triangle component. String the fourth wire through the center of the triangle.

3 On each of the wires, string a flat spacer, a rondelle, and a flat spacer.

4 On each of the three outer wires, string a corner hole of a triangle and a bicone. String the fourth wire through the center of the triangle. Over all four wires, string a flat spacer and a bicone.

1 earrings • Cut two 9-in. (23 cm) pieces of wire. Center an 11º seed bead over both wires. Over all four ends, string a bicone crystal.

2 Follow the directions for a square bead. Make a wrapped loop (Basics, p. 12) with all four wires.

3 Open the loop of an earring wire (Basics, p. 12). Attach the dangle and close the loop. Make a second earring.

Tip

Handle the earrings with care: you'll need 30-gauge wire to pass four strands through the bicone crystals, but it is delicate.

Design alternative

String only one seed bead between the "woven" beads for a lush look. Bicone crystals can be substituted for the rondelles.

Sew a
flower
necklace

Wielding a needle and
thread has never been
easier or more fashionable

by Aga Kruk

Use tulle
to make
fabric
flowers
like these.

Supplies

necklace 36–56 in. (.9–1.4 m)

- 3 x 36 in. (7.6 x 90 cm) fabric
- 4 yd. (3.6 m) 24- or 26-gauge wire
- 36–56 in. (.9–1.4 m) chain, 4–8 mm links
- **2** pairs of pliers (may include chainnose, roundnose, and/or bentnose)
- diagonal wire cutters
- grid ruler
- mandrel or pen
- rotary cutter and cutting mat
- sewing needle and thread

If you are a sewer, you probably already have the supplies for this necklace. If you're not, you will be after you see just how easy it is to make these elegant flowers. Choose your fabric first. The pink version has silver threads running through the fabric so I chose silver chain to match. For an edgier style, look for heavier gunmetal chain. Expand your options with an extra-long piece so you can wear the necklace doubled, asymmetrical, or knotted in the middle.

1 To make a fabric flower: Use a rotary cutter, a grid ruler, and a mat to cut a 3 x 18-in. (7.6 x 46 cm) strip of fabric.

2 Center a needle on a 36-in. (.9 m) length of thread. Fold the fabric in half lengthwise. Fold over one end and secure the fold with a stitch.

3 Turn the strip over and sew a running stitch along the two cut edges.

4 When you reach the end of the strip, pull the thread so the fabric bunches up. Shape the fabric into a flower. Secure all the layers by stitching them together.

5 Cut a 36–56-in. (.9–1.4 m) piece of chain. Open an end link (Basics, p. 12) and connect the other end. Close the link. Sew the flower to a link of chain by stitching through the flower and the link. Do not trim the thread; you will do so in step 9.

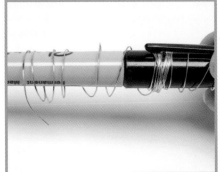

6 To make a wire bead: Cut a 36-in. (.9 m) piece of 24- or 26-gauge wire. Wrap the wire loosely around a mandrel or the barrel of a pen to form a long coil.

Design alternative

For a no-sew necklace, attach flower brooches to chain. Look for brooches in the beading section of your local craft store.

Customize your flowers

- Don't limit yourself to tulle. Try other fabric, netting, or even a nylon stocking.
- Vary the sizes of your finished flowers by cutting narrow or wide strips of fabric.
- The size of your finished wire bead depends on the size of the mandrel you use. For a 16 mm bead, use the barrel of a thick marker as your mandrel.
- Try thicker wire, or use sterling silver wire and oxidize your beads.

7 Remove the coil and form a ball by intertwining the coils and squeezing the ball between your fingers.

8 Cut a 36-in. (.9 m) piece of wire. Wrap the wire around the ball, occasionally anchoring it under another wire. Leave a 2-in. (5 cm) tail on each end.

9 With the thread from step 5, sew the wire ball through the center of the flower to the chain. Trim the thread. Poke the wire tails through the flower and wrap them around the link a few times. Trim the excess wire and tuck the ends.

10 Make another fabric flower and wire bead and attach them to the chain 10–16 in. (25–41 cm) from the first flower.

"Nature inspires me and I enjoy the challenge of re-creating its many shapes and forms." —Aga

Fall for FLOWERS

Make a flower work any time of year ◆ by Naomi Fujimoto

When I piled these cherry- and watermelon-colored Lucite beads on top of aquamarine nuggets, the combination looked fresh — a fun new palette to experiment with. So I wired the beads together and topped it all off with a vintage earring at the flower's center. Because the gemstones are an understated, versatile shade, I can wear the necklace even as the seasons and colors change.

Tip

I used oval jump rings in my earrings. Whether you use oval or round, make sure that the jump rings are 22-gauge or finer so they fit through the holes of the Lucite beads.

(1) bracelet • Cut a 7–9-in. (18–23 cm) piece of chain. Open a jump ring (Basics, p. 12). Attach an end link and a lobster claw clasp. Close the jump ring.

(2) Use a jump ring to attach a diamanté drop and an end link of chain. Use a jump ring to attach a flat polygon and a diamanté drop in a second color to the next link.

(4) On a head pin, string a bicone crystal, a gemstone nugget, and a bicone. Make the first half of a wrapped loop (Basics, p. 12). Attach the end link of chain and complete the wraps.

(3) Use jump rings to attach flat polygon and diamanté drops to links as desired. Leave the last link or two open.

134

necklace • Cut a piece of beading wire (Basics, p. 13). String an alternating pattern of bicone crystals and gemstone nuggets until the strand is within 3 in. (7.6 cm) of the finished length.

①

②

Cut a piece of beading wire 3 in. (7.6 cm) longer than the first. String an alternating pattern of bicones and nuggets until the strand is within 3 in. (7.6 cm) of the finished length.

Attach two-to-one connectors and a clasp (Technique, p. 137).

③

"I loved having the chance to mix colors I'm not used to working with."
—Naomi

④

Make a flower (Lucite flower, p. 136). Pin the flower to the outer strand.

Lucite flower

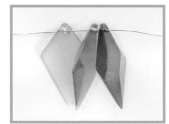

1 Cut a 24-in. (61 cm) piece of 26-gauge wire. String a flat polygon drop and two diamanté drops in different colors. Repeat seven times.

2 Twist the wire ends together so the beads make a tight circle. Trim the short end.

3 Wrap the wire between and around individual beads to reinforce the circle. Trim the excess wire and use chainnose pliers to tuck the end.

4 Cut a 20-in. (51 cm) piece of 26-gauge wire. String a mesh dome and the flower. Go back through the dome. Twist the wire ends together. Trim the short end.

5 Secure the flower to the dome by stitching the wire back and forth through both. Attach the flower near the edges of the dome; you'll need to attach the earring to the center in step 6. Trim the excess wire and use chainnose pliers to tuck the end.

6 Cut a 12-in. (30 cm) piece of 26-gauge wire. Flip open a clip-on earring. Attach the earring by stitching the wire back and forth through the earring's clip and the center holes of the dome. Trim the excess wire and use chainnose pliers to tuck the end.

7 Using chainnose pliers, attach the pin-back finding to the dome by bending the prongs inward.

Tip

- For the center of the flower, you can use a post earring instead of a clip-on. If you use a post, make sure to use one with filigree or other loops for attaching it to the dome.

---

earrings • Cut a nine-link piece of chain. Open a jump ring (Basics, p. 12). Attach a diamanté drop and an end link. Close the jump ring. Open the loop of an earring wire (Basics, p. 12). Attach the top link. Close the loop.

1

2

Two links from the bottom, use a jump ring to attach a polygon drop. Use jump rings to attach the remaining drops to every other link. Make a second earring the mirror image of the first.

1 On each end of each strand, string a crimp bead, a Wire Guardian, and the corresponding loop of a two-to-one connector. Go back through the crimp bead and the adjacent bead and tighten the wire. Check the fit, and add or remove beads if necessary. Don't over-tighten the wires; you'll need a tiny gap where you can pin the flower. Crimp the crimp beads (Basics, p. 13).

2 Open a jump ring (Basics, p. 12). On one end, attach the remaining loop of the connector and a hook clasp. Close the jump ring. Repeat on the other end, substituting a 3-in. (7.6 cm) piece of chain for the clasp.

3 On a head pin, string a bicone crystal, a gemstone nugget, and a bicone. Make the first half of a wrapped loop (Basics, p. 12). Attach the end link of chain and complete the wraps.

4 If desired, close a crimp cover over each crimp.

Supplies

necklace 19–20½ in. (48–52.1 cm)
- **2** 16-in. (41 cm) strands 17–27 mm faceted gemstone nuggets
- **16** 33 mm Lucite diamanté drops, in two colors
- **8** 32 mm Lucite flat polygon drops
- **34–44** 3 mm bicone crystals, in three colors
- flexible beading wire, .018 or .019
- 56 in. (1.4 m) 26-gauge wire
- 19–23 mm clip-on earring
- ⅞-in. (22 mm) mesh dome with pin-back finding
- **2** two-to-one connectors
- 1½-in. (3.8 cm) head pin
- **2** 6–7 mm jump rings
- **4** crimp beads
- **4** crimp covers (optional)
- **4** Wire Guardians
- hook clasp

- 3 in. (7.6 cm) chain for extender, 12 mm links
- chainnose and roundnose pliers
- diagonal wire cutters
- crimping pliers (optional)

bracelet
- **9–13** 33 mm Lucite diamanté drops, in two colors
- **8–12** 32 mm Lucite flat polygon drops
- 17–20 mm faceted gemstone nugget, left over from necklace
- **2** 3 mm bicone crystals
- 7–9 in. (18–23 cm) chain, 12 mm links
- 1½-in. (3.8 cm) head pin
- **17–25** 6–7 mm jump rings
- lobster claw clasp
- chainnose and roundnose pliers
- diagonal wire cutters

earrings
- **6** 33 mm Lucite diamanté drops, 4 in one color, 2 in another
- **4** 32 mm Lucite flat polygon drops
- 3 in. (7.6 cm) chain, 4 mm links
- **10** 6–7 mm jump rings
- pair of earring wires
- chainnose and roundnose pliers, or **2** pairs of chainnose pliers
- diagonal wire cutters

Double vis

Make a reversible pendant with an open-back bezel and ICE resin

by Susan Lenart Kazmer

I love the opportunities an open-back bezel offers — even if it does come with challenges. For my clown pendant, I flipped the bezel upside down and drilled two holes for a handmade wire bail. But for a first foray into filling open-back bezels with resin, you can simplify the process and skip the bail. The most important thing: Don't expect expert results from your first attempts. For some tips, check out the list of do's and don'ts (p. 140) before you get started.

1 pendant • Cut a piece of packing tape to fit over the back of an open-back bezel. Press the tape along the back of the bezel. Use a craft stick to burnish the tape to create a tight seal.

Cut two images to fit back-to-back in the bezel. Using a sponge applicator, coat each side of each image with Mod Podge and allow to dry for about six hours.

2 Following the manufacturer's directions, mix a small batch of ICE Resin.

Place the bezel on a flat surface. Using the tip of the craft stick, drip resin to cover the bottom ¼ of the bezel.

3 Place an image face down in the bezel. Slowly drip resin in the bezel. Place another image face up in the bezel.

For a shallow bezel, drip resin to the top. Allow to fully cure for three days. Remove the tape from the back of the bezel.

For a deep bezel, drip resin until the bezel is ¾ full. Allow to dry. Mix a new batch of resin. Drip resin to the top of the bezel. Allow to cure. Remove the tape.

on

Cut a 2-in. (5 cm) piece of bronze wire. Hammer or ball each end. Center a button on a 50–58-in. (1.3–1.5 m) piece of leather. Wrap the wire around both halves of the leather to secure the button.

4

Cut a 4-in. (10 cm) piece of bronze wire. Hammer or ball each end. Attach the pendant to both pieces of leather.

6

5

Fill a light bulb bezel with E6000. Insert the leather ends and allow to dry. Open a jump ring (Basics, p. 12) and attach a hook clasp. Close the jump ring.

3

Visit artjewelrymag .com to learn to use a flex shaft for drilling.

Visit *Art Jewelry*'s website, artjewelrymag. com/videos, to watch the "Balling the End of Wire" video.

2

1

necklace •
Make a pendant (previous page). Use a permanent marker to personalize the image before coating it with Mod Podge.

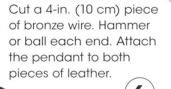

Do:

- Use a craft stick to burnish the back of the taped bezel (photo 1).

- After slowly and thoroughly mixing the resin for two minutes, allow it to sit for five minutes before dripping it into the bezel.

- Layer the images close to the surface of each side of a deep bezel (photo 2).

- Use images with a lot of contrast. Otherwise, especially in a deep pendant, the details get lost.

- Pour the bezel almost full and let the resin dry for six hours. Resin in a deep bezel will overflow if you try to dome it in one pour. Mix up a new batch of resin and drip in a layer to dome.

Don't:

- Pour resin into the bezel directly from a cup. Instead, drip small amounts of resin from the tip of a craft stick (photo 3).

- Wait to clean up spilled resin. You have 30 to 45 minutes before it starts to harden (photo 4).

For more tips and techniques, visit iceresin.com.

Supplies

pendant
- 15–45 mm bezel with loop
- diagonal wire cutters
- ICE Resin
- Mod Podge
- images to fit inside bezel
- mixing cups
- packing tape
- plastic gloves
- safety goggles
- sponge applicators
- waxed paper
- wooden craft sticks

necklace 28 in. (71 cm)
- pendant
- 18 mm glass button
- 50–58 in. (1.3–1.5 m) 2 mm leather cord
- 6 in (15 cm) 18-gauge bronze wire
- 6 mm light bulb bezel
- hook clasp
- 9 mm jump ring
- **2** pairs of pliers
- E6000 adhesive
- hammer
- bench block or anvil

Glass button by Michele Goldstein, michelegoldstein.com.

Design alternatives

Try different bezel styles. These square frame bezels are perfect for lightweight earrings.

Unearthed
elements

Combine rugged art beads
and metallic nuggets for
an ancient aesthetic

by Gretchen McHale

I found inspiration for this bracelet in Heather Wynn's polymer clay beads. They look like they could have been relics from an Egyptian tomb, so I wanted to create a piece with the feel of ancient jewelry. That's where the metal-coated resin nuggets came in. I love working with these nuggets because they look like huge statement pieces, but the beads are really light so they don't weigh the design down.

Supplies

bracelet
- **2–3** 20–25 mm metallic resin nuggets
- **2–3** 13–18 mm art beads
- **12–14** 8–10 mm teardrop-shaped pearls
- **24–28** 4 mm bicone crystals in four colors
- 8º seed beads (optional)
- **10–24** 4–6 mm flat spacers
- 15–18 in. (38–46 cm) 20-gauge wire
- **36–42** 1½-in. (3.8 cm) head pins
- **6–7** 8–10 mm jump rings
- **2** 5–6 mm jump rings
- toggle clasp
- chainnose and roundnose pliers
- diagonal wire cutters

earrings
- **2** 13–18 mm art beads
- **8** 4 mm bicone crystals in four colors
- **4–8** 4–6 mm flat spacers
- **8** 1½-in. (3.8 cm) head pins
- 3½ in. (8.9 cm) chain, 9–10 mm (medium) links
- 3 in. (7.6 cm) chain, 3–4 mm (small) links
- **2** 2-in. (5 cm) head pins
- pair of earring wires
- chainnose and roundnose pliers
- diagonal wire cutters

Polymer clay beads by Heather Wynn, heatherwynn.com. Metallic resin beads from The Bead Goes On, thebeadgoeson.com. Copper-glazed raku beads by Keith O'Connor, eebeads.com.

1 bracelet • Cut a 3-in. (7.6 cm) piece of wire. Make a wrapped loop (Basics, p. 12) on one end. String one or two spacers, an art bead, and one or two spacers. Make a wrapped loop. Make two or three art-bead units and two or three resin-nugget units.

2 On a head pin, string a pearl. Make a wrapped loop. Make 12 to 14 pearl units and 24 to 28 crystal units.

3 Open an 8–10 mm jump ring (Basics, p. 12) and attach: art-bead unit, crystal unit, pearl unit, crystal unit, resin-nugget unit, crystal unit, pearl unit, crystal unit. Close the jump ring. Continue attaching bead units with 8–10 mm jump rings.

4 On each end, use an 8–10 mm jump ring to attach four crystal units and two pearl units. Use a 5–6 mm jump ring to attach half of a toggle clasp.

> **"**The way the bead colors come together with the crystals and pearls turns a simple bracelet into a complex work of art with lots of depth.**"** –Gretchen

1 earrings • On a 2-in. (5 cm) head pin, string one or two spacers, an art bead, and one or two spacers. Make the first half of a wrapped loop (Basics, p. 12).

2 Cut a 1½-in. (3.8 cm) piece of medium-link chain. Attach the art-bead unit to one end and complete the wraps.

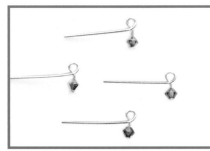

3 On a 1½-in. (3.8 cm) head pin, string a bicone crystal. Make the first half of a wrapped loop. Make four crystal units.

4 Cut a 1¼-in. (3.2 cm) piece of small-link chain. Attach a crystal unit to one end and complete the wraps. Attach the remaining crystal units to the chain, skipping one link between each.

5 Open the loop of an earring wire (Basics, p. 12) and attach the dangles. Close the loop. Make a second earring.

Tips

- The resin nuggets have large holes, as do many art beads. To stabilize the wire inside the nugget and art-bead units, I strung 8º seed beads in the holes.
- Metallic resin nuggets are available in bright copper, old copper, bright gold, Dutch gold, bright silver, and pewter finishes. They also come in 10 x 14 mm (mini) size.

Design alternative

To create an organic look in a necklace, use leather to suspend a centerpiece of resin nuggets or art beads.

Link stiffened WireLace in a mixed media necklace

by Elizabeth Del Monte

③ On each end, use a 10 mm jump ring to attach the bead unit and an 8–14 in. (20–36 mm) piece of chain.

Reinforced
with resin

As I was forming WireLace into organic shapes, it occurred to me to use resin to preserve the ones I liked. I chose beads to mimic the colors in the pendant, which can be opened and embellished with cutouts from cards or fabric. Balance your multi-component piece by making the connectors, bead units, and WireLace links about the same length.

Supplies

WireLace links
- 12 in. (30 cm) WireLace, 20 mm wide
- hole punch, ⅛- or ¹⁄₁₆-in. diameter
- ICE Resin
- mixing cups
- plastic gloves
- safety goggles
- scissors
- sponge applicators
- waxed paper
- wooden craft sticks

necklace 18 in. (46 cm)
- **5** WireLace links
- 45 mm pendant
- **12–20** 12–16 mm beads
- 30 mm beaded connector
- **20–24** 4–14 mm spacers

- 8–14 in. (20–36 cm) chain, 20 mm links
- 12 in. (30 cm) 18-gauge wire
- 30 in. (76 cm) 24-gauge wire
- **2** 10 mm jump rings
- **5** 5 mm jump rings
- chainnose and roundnose pliers
- diagonal wire cutters
- pen

earrings
- **2** WireLace links
- **2** 12–16 mm beads
- **4** 4 mm flat spacers
- 7 in. (18 cm) 24-gauge wire
- pair of earring wires
- chainnose and roundnose pliers
- diagonal wire cutters

2 On each side, use 5 mm jump rings and wire connectors to attach bead units and WireLace links.

66This necklace is the perfect length to show the balance of subtle and bright colors and is still wearable.99
—Elizabeth

Tip

Resin may change the color of your WireLace. I used chocolate WireLace and the resin deepened the color to almost black.

necklace • Make WireLace links, wire connectors, and bead units. (p. 146). Open a 5 mm jump ring (Basics, p. 12) and attach a pendant and a bead unit. Close the jump ring. Use a 5 mm jump ring to attach another bead unit to the pendant.

1

I cut out a card and inserted it between the plastic and glass of this two-sided pendant.

1 WireLace links • Cut five 2-in. (5 cm) piece of WireLace. Use your fingers to pull and shape each piece as desired.

2 Mix resin according to the manufacturer's instructions. Place the WireLace pieces on waxed paper. Use a sponge applicator to apply resin to one side of each WireLace piece. Allow to dry. Apply resin to the other side of each piece and allow to dry.

3 Use a hole punch to punch a hole about ⅛ in. (3 mm) from the edge of each piece. Punch a second hole across from the first.

1 wire connectors • Leaving the 18-gauge wire on the spool, pull one end around the barrel of a pen. Place your roundnose pliers next to the loop and pull the wire around the largest part of your roundnose pliers.

2 Trim the ends of the wire to make an S.

3 Grasp each loop with pliers. Bring one pair of pliers toward you so the loops are perpendicular. Make ten wire links.

bead units • Cut a 3-in. (7.6 cm) piece of 24-gauge wire. Make a wrapped loop (Basics, p. 12) on one end. String beads and spacers and make a wrapped loop. Make ten bead units.

① earrings • For each earring: Make a WireLace link (above), punching only one hole. Cut a 3½-in. (8.9 cm) piece of wire. Use the largest part of your roundnose pliers to make the first half of a wrapped loop (Basics, p. 12). Attach the WireLace link and complete the wraps.

② String a spacer, a bead, and a spacer. Make a wrapped loop perpendicular to the first. Open the loop of an earring wire (Basics, p. 12) and attach the dangle. Close the loop.

Grow your earring collection

String Lucite flowers and leaves for no-fail earrings

by Lori Anderson

This earring design is so easy, you won't be able to stop after making just one pair. Combine flowers and leaves in different shapes and sizes, or try a variety of bead caps and crystals at the center of each flower. You'll be delighted with every bud that blooms.

1 On a head pin, string a bicone crystal, a flower bead, and a leaf bead. Make a right-angle bend in back of the leaf.

2 String three spacers and a bicone. Make a wrapped loop (Basics, p. 12).

3 Open the loop of an earring wire (Basics, p. 12). Attach the dangle and close the loop. Make a second earring.

Supplies

- ◆ **2** 19 mm Lucite leaf beads
- ◆ **2** 14 mm Lucite flower beads
- ◆ **4** 4 mm bicone crystals
- ◆ **6** 3 mm flat spacers
- ◆ **2** 2-in. (5 cm) head pins
- ◆ pair of earring wires
- ◆ chainnose and roundnose pliers
- ◆ diagonal wire cutters

Neutral ground

Wood beads provide a framework for vibrant color

by Jane Konkel

These smooth, shapely wood beads are lightweight, and their neutral tones make them the perfect background for doses of bright color. Look for achromatic shades like grey, ivory, beige, brown, or oatmeal, and add a vibrant accent like aqua, purple, coral, fuchsia, or turquoise. You'll love designing using this basic color scheme.

1 Cut a 2-in. (5 cm) piece of 24-gauge wire and make a plain loop (Basics, p. 12). String a spacer, an oval bead, and a spacer. Make a plain loop. Make four oval units.

2 Cut a 3-in. (7.6 cm) piece of 20-gauge wire. Make a plain loop. String a wood bead and make a plain loop.

Supplies

- **2** 30 mm wood beads, top drilled
- **8** 5 mm oval beads
- **16** 4 mm flat spacers
- 6 in. (15 cm) 20-gauge wire
- 16 in. (41 cm) 24-gauge wire
- 4 in. (10 cm) chain, 3–4 mm links
- pair of earring wires
- chainnose and roundnose pliers
- diagonal wire cutters

3 Cut three pieces of chain, each three links long. Open a loop of an oval unit (Basics, p. 12) and attach a piece of chain. Close the loop. Continue attaching the remaining oval units and chain.

4 On each end of the chain segment, attach a loop of the wood-bead unit.

5 Attach the loop of an earring wire and the center link of the chain segment. Make a second earring.

149

Newfangled bangle

Capture beads or found objects in a playful resin bangle

by Sherri Haab

Fun and bright, these bracelets make great homes for your favorite beads and bits. My first bangles were inspired by apple juice Bakelite bangles, which often include floral designs. I had a collection of vintage plastic, and the small pieces fit nicely into a bangle mold. After you master the basic bangle, play with colorants to make striped layers.

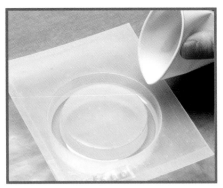

1 Following the manufacturer's directions, mix ½ ounce each of resin and hardener in a cup. Place the mold on a flat surface. Pour the resin into the bangle mold about half full. Briefly hold a heat gun over the resin to gently remove any bubbles. Use the heat gun again after a few minutes if any bubbles remain.

2 Wait until the resin thickens slightly, then place beads and found objects using pliers or tweezers. Allow to cure. You can speed the curing process by placing the mold near a 60- to 100-watt light bulb. Resin is fully cured when it is tack free and hard to the touch.

3 Mix ½ ounce each of resin and hardener in a cup and pour it into the mold. Add another layer of beads or found objects and allow to cure.

Supplies

- **15–70** 4–20 mm beads or found objects
- EasyCast Clear Casting Epoxy resin
- bangle mold
- mixing cups
- plastic gloves
- safety goggles
- chainnose or bentnose pliers or tweezers
- emery board, metal file, or 200-grit sandpaper
- heat gun
- wet/dry sandpapers in 320, 400, 600, 800, 1000, and 1200 grits
- wooden craft sticks
- buffing compounds, lathe and muslin buffing wheels (optional)

Tips

- To avoid bubbles, warm the resin and hardener before working. Set the bottles under a light bulb or in a warm place.
- If you use large (20 mm) beads, make sure they're flat; otherwise they won't fit in the bangle.
- In step 2, make sure to wait until the resin has thickened before you add beads or objects. If you add them too soon, they'll sink to the bottom.
- The mold is reusable, so flex it back into shape after removing the finished bracelet.

Polishing option

For a crystal clear finish, use buffing compounds on a muslin wheel. Start with a cutting compound and a stitched wheel at a low speed (1000–1500 rpm). Use an unstitched wheel with a polishing compound for a final buff. For more information, visit foredom.net.

4 To remove the bangle, flex the mold and push on the back to gently loosen the bangle. Push the center of the mold inward (almost inside out) to free one of the edges.

5 To remove the rough edge at the top of the bangle, sand it with 200-grit sandpaper or an emery board.

6 Continue sanding the bangle in a bowl of water using wet/dry sandpapers. Sand the top and inside edges with 320, 400, 600, 800, 1000, and 1200 grit papers, in that order. Use fresh water after each paper. Polish the bangle if desired (Polishing option, above).

MOLD
a bold pendant

Resin, gilders paste, and paint add dimension to brass stampings

by Brenda Schweder

Brass stampings are the foundation of this project — both literally and figuratively. I was first inspired by the intricate details of the components, so I used them to create a mold. Later, they served as the actual backing for the molded resin. The key is to choose a stamping with a deep well. Adding a dab of oil paint to the resin created the first layer of color. Applications of gilders paste and ink gave the piece even more depth. I kept the stringing (and matching earrings) simple to let the pendant be the focus.

Supplies

pendant
- brass stamping with a deep well
- ¾ in. (1.9 cm) 22-gauge wire
- Adirondack ink
- gilders paste
- oil paint
- two-part epoxy adhesive
- two-part epoxy resin
- two-part mold material
- mixing cups
- plastic gloves
- safety goggles
- hammer and bench block or anvil
- soft cloth
- wooden craft sticks
- sponge applicator (optional)

scarab necklace 18 in. (46 cm)
- scarab pendant
- **30–40** assorted 6–8 mm beads
- **160–180** 3 mm heishi beads
- flexible beading wire, .014 or .015

- **2** 10 mm jump rings
- **2** crimp beads
- S-hook clasp and two soldered jump rings
- **2** pairs of pliers
- diagonal wire cutters
- crimping pliers (optional)

owl necklace 18 in. (46 cm)
- owl pendant
- **3** 16-in. (41 cm) strands 4 mm olive wood beads
- **38–44** 4 mm round pearls
- **8–20** 3 mm bicone crystals
- 52 mm loop bail, with two holes
- flexible beading wire, .014 or .015
- 7 mm jump ring
- **8** crimp beads
- **2** crimp covers
- toggle clasp
- chainnose or crimping pliers
- diagonal wire cutters

earrings
- **2** 14 mm quatrefoil links
- **4** 4 mm olive wood beads
- **2** 4 mm round pearls
- **2** 7 mm jump rings
- **6** 1½-in. (3.8 cm) head pins
- pair of earring wires
- chainnose and roundnose pliers
- diagonal wire cutters

Scarab stamping from B'sue Boutiques, bsueboutiques.com. Owl stamping and bail from The Mermaids Dowry, mermaidsdowry.etsy.com. Olive wood beads from Silk Road Treasures, silkroadtreasures.com.

4

On each end, string a crimp bead, a heishi, and a soldered jump ring. Check the fit, allowing for the clasp, and add or remove beads if necessary. Go back through the beads just strung and tighten the wire. Crimp the crimp bead (Basics, p. 12) and trim the excess wire. Attach an S-hook clasp to one of the jump rings.

3

On each end, string heishi beads until the strand is within 1 in. (2.5 cm) of the finished length.

2

Cut a 24–26-in. (61–66 cm) piece of beading wire. Center a 6–8 mm bead. On each end, string 3½ in. (8.9 cm) of 6–8 mm beads.

> "Once I ironed out the mechanical details of this technique, I had a blast with the creative possibilities it offers." –Brenda

1

scarab necklace • Make the pendant (p. 155), but skip step 5.

5

Open two jump rings (Basics, p. 12). Attach the pendant and close the jump rings.

Supply note

If possible, buy two stampings; you can save time and fill both halves of the pendant at once.

Color note

For the scarab pendant, I used viridian blue and titanium white paint and copper ink to tint the resin. Then I applied iris blue, antique gold, and cream gilders paste.

Tip

Once you're comfortable with the molding process, consider making the bail first and pressing it into the mold material to encase it in the poured resin.

1 owl necklace • Make a pendant (p. 155).

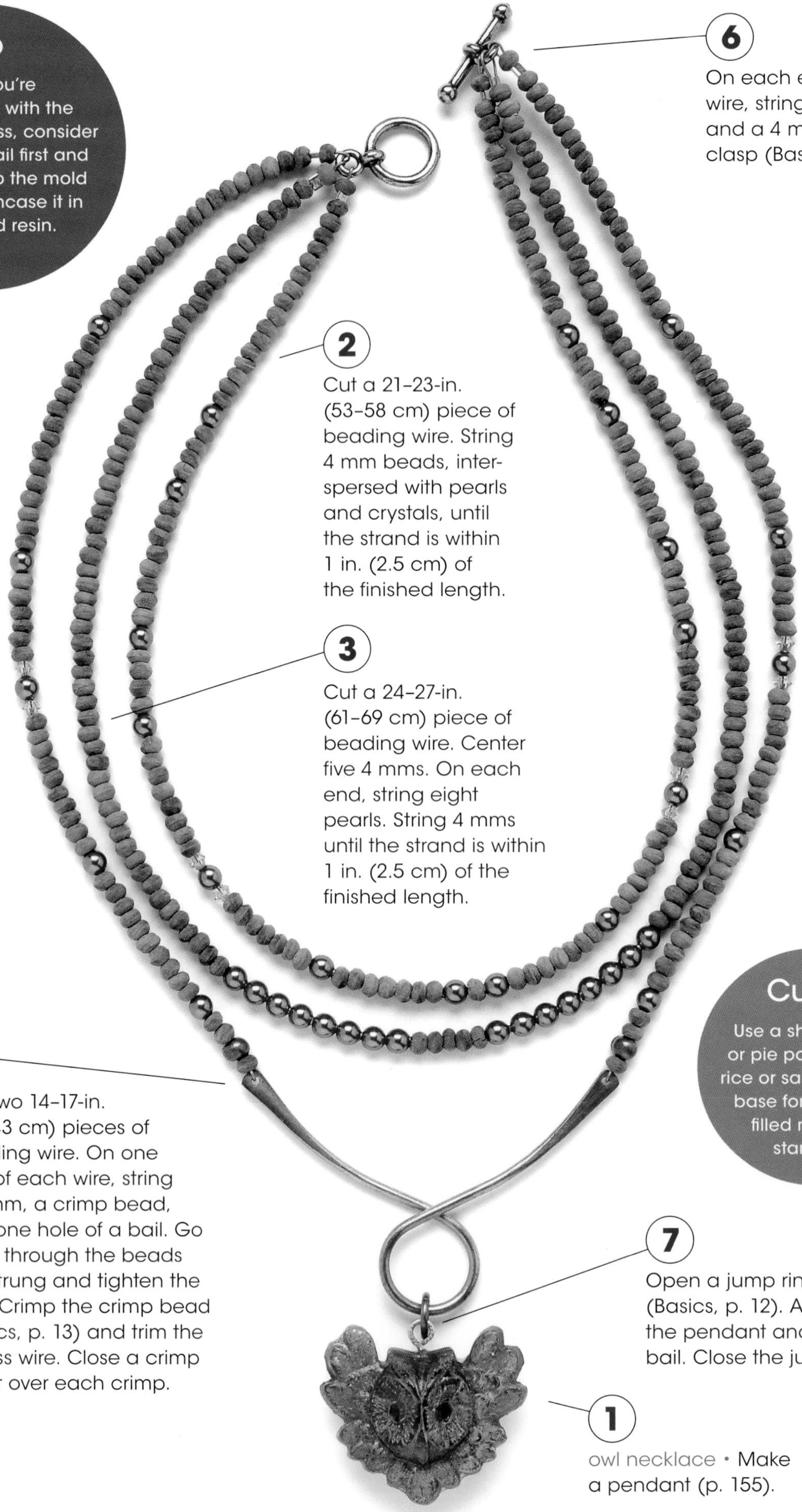

2 Cut a 21–23-in. (53–58 cm) piece of beading wire. String 4 mm beads, interspersed with pearls and crystals, until the strand is within 1 in. (2.5 cm) of the finished length.

3 Cut a 24–27-in. (61–69 cm) piece of beading wire. Center five 4 mms. On each end, string eight pearls. String 4 mms until the strand is within 1 in. (2.5 cm) of the finished length.

4 Cut two 14–17-in. (34–43 cm) pieces of beading wire. On one end of each wire, string a 4 mm, a crimp bead, and one hole of a bail. Go back through the beads just strung and tighten the wire. Crimp the crimp bead (Basics, p. 13) and trim the excess wire. Close a crimp cover over each crimp.

5 On each wire, string 4 mms, interspersed with pearls and crystals, until the strand is within 1 in. (2.5 cm) of the finished length.

6 On each end of each wire, string a crimp bead and a 4 mm, and add a clasp (Basics, p. 13).

7 Open a jump ring (Basics, p. 12). Attach the pendant and the bail. Close the jump ring.

Curing

Use a shallow bowl or pie pan filled with rice or sand as a level base for your resin-filled mold and stamping.

1 pendant • To make the first half of the pendant: Follow the manufacturer's directions to prepare the mold. Press the stamping into the mold deep enough to create a narrow lip.

2 Let the mold set for 20 minutes. Remove the stamping.

3 Follow manufacturer's directions to prepare the resin. Add a drop (about 5 mm) of oil paint and a drop or two of ink. Mix well and let the resin de-gas for several minutes. Making sure the mold is level, drip in resin just to the edge of the design. Allow to cure.

4 To make the other half of the pendant: Be sure the stamping is level, and fill it just to the edge. Do not dome the resin. Allow to cure.

5 Cut a ¾-in. (1.9 cm) piece of 22-gauge wire. Make a plain loop (Basics, p. 12). Hammer the stem to make a flatter surface to sandwich between the resin halves.

6 Remove the cured resin from the mold. With a little resin or adhesive, glue the halves with the bail centered between them. Let dry.

7 Use a sponge applicator or your finger to apply gilders paste and ink to the resin as desired, then buff with a soft cloth.

Design alternative

I added tiny watch parts to this pear casting and encased it in a wire cage and bail.

1 earrings • For each earring: On a head pin, string a 4 mm bead and make the first half of a wrapped loop (Basics, p. 12). Make two 4 mm units and a pearl unit. Attach each bead unit to a link and complete the wraps.

2 Open a jump ring (Basics, p. 12). Attach the dangle and the loop of an earring wire. Close the jump ring.

Mix metallic colors in a classic design.

String three strands
in kindred colors

Combine colors with confidence

by Christianne Camera

If you're new to combining colors, try mixing different intensities of the same hue. Or for a slightly trickier mix, choose a harmonious blend of different colors that are similar in tone and intensity. Select two strands of 6 mm beads and one strand that's a little smaller. Any round beads will work, but I like these inexpensive textured ones. Seeing the strands hang side by side will help you choose a palette of compatible colors.

1 necklace • Cut three pieces of beading wire (Basics, p. 12). On two wires, string alternating 6 mm beads and 11º seed beads until the strands are within 2 in. (5 cm) of the finished length. On the remaining wire, string alternating 4 mm beads and 11ºs until the strand is within 2 in. (5 cm) of the finished length.

2 On each end of the 4 mm strand, string a crimp bead and the middle loop of a clasp. On each end of the 6 mm strands, string a crimp bead and an outer loop of the clasp. Go back through the last few beads strung. Check the fit, and add or remove beads if necessary. Tighten the wires and crimp the crimp beads (Basics, p. 13).

Supplies

necklace 18 in. (46 cm)
- **2** 16-in. (41 cm) strands 6 mm round beads, in two colors
- 16-in. (41 cm) strand 4 mm round beads, in a third color
- 5 g 11º seed beads
- flexible beading wire, .010 or .012
- **6** crimp beads
- three-strand clasp
- chainnose or crimping pliers
- diagonal wire cutters

earrings
- **8** 6 mm round beads, in two colors
- **4** 4 mm round beads, in a third color
- **12** 11º seed beads
- 1 in. (2.5 cm) chain, 3–4 mm links
- **12** 1½-in. (3.8 cm) head pins
- pair of earring wires
- chainnose and roundnose pliers
- diagonal wire cutters

1 earrings • On a head pin, string a 6 mm bead and an 11º seed bead. Make the first half of a wrapped loop (Basics, p. 12). Make four 6 mm bead units (two in each color) and two 4 mm bead units.

2 Cut a ½-in. (1.3 cm) piece of chain. Open the loop of an earring wire (Basics, p. 12) and attach the chain. Close the loop.

Tip

If you want the beads to be anchored while you string, attach half of the clasp on one end of each wire first.

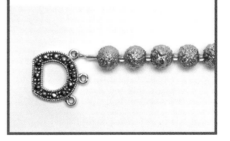

3 Attach a 4 mm and two 6 mm bead units to the bottom link. Complete the wraps as you go.

4 Attach the remaining bead units to the top link. Make a second earring.

Hedge your fashion bets

Take a novelty bead from cute to current

by Jamie Hogsett

This hedgehog bead is irresistible, but how do you get from aww to awesome? A cute bead can be a perfect focal piece for a fashionable necklace, the trick is using stylish and sophisticated accent beads and findings to keep the cuteness in the proper proportion. Start with Heather Powers' adorable hedgie bead and attach richly colored disk beads and etched metal links, and use two hooks for an asymmetrical clasp.

Pewter hooks and links add a swirly complement to earthy disk beads.

Supplies

necklace 17 in. (43 cm)
- 25 mm hedgehog bead
- **10–12** 12 mm disk beads, **6–7** in one color and **4–5** in another
- **20–24** 4 mm spacers
- **3** 33 mm pewter links
- flexible beading wire, .014 or .015
- **6** 5–6 mm jump rings
- 2-in. (5 cm) head pin
- **20–24** crimp beads
- **20–24** crimp covers
- **2** 24 mm hooks
- chainnose and roundnose pliers

- crimping pliers
- diagonal wire cutters

earrings
- **2** 12 mm disk beads
- **2** 6 mm rondelles
- **2** 7 mm spacers
- **2** 6 mm spacers
- **2** 10 mm rings
- **2** 2-in. (5 cm) head pins
- pair of earring wires
- chainnose and roundnose pliers
- diagonal wire cutters

Polymer clay hedgehog and disk beads from Humble Beads, humblebeads.com. Pewter links and hooks from Green Girl Studios, greengirlstudios.com.

1 necklace • On a head pin, string a hedgehog bead and make a wrapped loop (Basics, p. 12). Set aside for step 7.

2 Cut a 3-in. (7.6 cm) piece of beading wire. String a crimp bead and a hook. Go back through the crimp bead and make a folded crimp (Basics, p. 13). Close a crimp cover over the crimp.

Design alternative

Heather Powers makes a variety of whimsical polymer clay critters. Here disk and gnome beads were used, along with links of copper chain.

3 a String: spacer, color A disk bead, spacer, crimp bead, hole of a link.

b Go back through the last beads strung and tighten the wire. Crimp the crimp bead and trim the excess wire. Close a crimp cover over the crimp.

4 To make a disk unit: On a 3-in. (7.6 cm) piece of beading wire, string the other hole of the link and a crimp bead. Repeat step 3b. String: spacer, color B disk, spacer, crimp bead, jump ring. Repeat step 3b.

5 Use five 3-in. (7.6 cm) pieces of beading wire to make and attach two color A disk units, one color B disk unit, and two color A units.

6 Use three 3-in. (7.6 cm) pieces of beading wire to make and attach: color B unit, link, color A unit, link, color B unit.

Tip

Use crimping pliers to gently close crimp covers over folded crimps.

7 Open the last jump ring (Basics, p. 12). Attach the hedgehog unit and a color B unit. Close the jump ring. Attach a hook as in step 2.

1 earrings • On a head pin, string a 6 mm spacer, a disk bead, a 7 mm spacer, and a 6 mm rondelle. Use the largest part of your roundnose pliers to make the first half of a wrapped loop (Basics, p. 12).

2 Attach a 10 mm ring and complete the wraps.

3 Open the loop of an earring wire (Basics, p. 12) and attach the dangle. Close the loop. Make a second earring.

Island necklace

by Jane Konkel

Concentrate seed and nut beads on one end of tropical-colored ribbons

To mimic your laid-back style, tie the ends asymmetrically. This necklace comes together so quickly, you'll have plenty of time to contemplate the easy breezy days ahead.

Tip

You can easily slide the rings up and down the ribbons to change the look.

1 On a head pin, string a spacer, a round bead, and a ring's hole. Make a right angle bend close to the bead. Using the largest part of your roundnose pliers, grasp the wire's tip and roll the wire to form a coil. Make 14 to 16 bead units.

2 Over two ribbons, string the bead units in alternating colors. Use your roundnose pliers to pull the ribbons through the bead units' loops. Position the bead units on the ribbons.

3 On a head pin, string a spacer and a paper bead. Make four paper-bead units with coils as in step 1. On each end of each ribbon, string a paper-bead unit and tie an overhand knot (Basics, p. 12).

Seeds and nuts

Saging saging are seed pods that come from plants found in the Philippines. The hard, hollow shells are sun-dried, sliced, and hand drilled. The salwag beads are carved from the nuts of salwag palm trees.

Supplies

necklace 16–21 in. (41–53 cm)

- 16-in. (41 cm) strand 18–28 mm saging-saging rings
- **4** 12–14 mm paper beads
- **14–16** 6 mm salwag round beads, in two colors
- **18–20** 4 mm spacers
- **2** 30–36-in. (.76–.9 m) silk ribbons
- **18–20** 1½-in. (3.8 cm) head pins
- roundnose pliers

Rings and round beads from Beads and Pieces, beadsandpieces.com. Paper beads from Bead for Life, beadforlifestore.org.

Nefertiti
necklace

Make a necklace befitting an Egyptian queen

by Nina Lara Novikova

I am fascinated with ancient Egypt's history and culture. The colors and gemstones used in ancient Egyptian jewelry have always impressed me. Cool deep blue lapis, warm bright blue turquoise, and deep red carnelian in combination with gold is striking. Every time I wear my Nefertiti necklace, the compliments make me feel like royalty.

Supplies

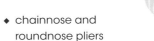

necklace 17½ in. (44.5 cm)
- **3** 10 mm flat square metal beads
- **8** 9 mm flat round metal beads
- 16-in. (41 cm) strand 9 mm oval beads
- 16-in. (41 cm) strand 4 mm cube beads
- 16-in. (41 cm) strand 4 mm round beads
- 16-in. (41 cm) strand 3 mm round beads
- **134–142** 2 mm spacers
- 8 ft. (2.4 m) 26-gauge wire
- 6 ft. (1.8 m) chain, 2 mm links
- **2** 6 mm split rings
- toggle clasp

- chainnose and roundnose pliers
- diagonal wire cutters
- split-ring pliers

earrings
- **2** 10 mm flat square metal beads
- **2** 4 mm cube beads
- **2** 4 mm round beads
- **2** 3 mm round beads
- **4** 2 mm spacers
- **2** 2-in. (5 cm) head pins
- pair of earring wires
- chainnose and roundnose pliers
- diagonal wire cutters

5 Leave nine to 12 links on each end and trim the excess chain. On each side, use a split ring (Basics, p. 12) to attach each end of chain and half of a clasp.

4 Make and attach cube-bead units (Components, p. 164) as shown.

1 necklace • Cut one 12-in. (30 cm) and three 18-in. (46 cm) pieces of chain.

"Once you see the jewelry in your imagination, the other steps are easy." —Nina

3 Make and attach oval-, round-, and square-bead units (Components, p. 164) as shown. Trim the excess from each end of the 12-in. (30 cm) chain.

2 Make a square-bead unit and attach the center link of each chain (Components, p. 164).

Components

For each bead unit: Cut a 1½-in. (3.8 cm) piece of wire. Make a small loop on one end.

square-bead unit • String a spacer and a square bead.

String a link of the 12-in. (30 cm) chain, a cube bead, and a link of an 18-in. (46 cm) chain.

String a 4 mm round bead and a link of another 18-in. (46 cm) chain.

String a 3 mm round bead and a link of another 18-in. (46 cm) chain.

String a spacer. Make a small loop.

oval-bead unit • String a spacer and an oval bead.

On each end of the necklace, skip four links from the previous unit and string the fifth link of the 12-in. (30 cm) chain. String a cube. Skip three links and string the fourth link of the next chain.

String a 4 mm round. Skip three links and string the fourth link of the next chain.

String a 3 mm round. Skip three links and string the fourth link of the next chain.

String a spacer. Make a small loop.

round-bead unit • String a spacer and a flat round metal bead.

On each end of the necklace, skip four links from the previous unit and string the fifth link of the 12-in. (30 cm) chain. String a cube. Skip three links and string the fourth link of the next chain.

String a 4 mm round. Skip three links and string the fourth link of the next chain.

String a 3 mm round. Skip three links and string the fourth link of the next chain.

String a spacer. Make a small loop.

Design alternative

Try a simpler version using bigger beads and chain with larger links.

cube-bead unit • String a spacer and a cube.

On each end of the necklace, skip three links from the previous unit and string the fourth link of the outside chain.

String a 4 mm round. Skip three links and string the fourth link of the inner chain.

String a 3 mm round. Skip three links and string the fourth link of the next chain.

String a spacer. Make a small loop.

1 earrings • On a head pin, string: 2 mm spacer, square bead, cube bead, 4 mm round bead, 3 mm round, 2 mm spacer. Make a wrapped loop (Basics, p. 12).

2 Open the loop of an earring wire (Basics, p. 12). Attach the dangle and close the loop. Make a second earring.

Accessorize with
APPLIQUÉ

Getting the look of handmade is easy if you have the notions

by Linda Gunderman

Even if you're all thumbs with a needle and thread, you can still make fashionable jewelry with a hand-sewn look. Instead of using a focal bead or fabric flowers at the center of my piece, I attached a pre-made appliqué that I picked up from the fabric section of my craft store. Just string a simple pattern of pearls, crystals, and spacers and you're done. So easy and current.

1 necklace • Use a micro-hole punch to punch a hole in an upper corner of an appliqué. Open a jump ring (Basics, p. 12) and attach the punched hole. Close the jump ring. Repeat on the other corner.

2 Cut a 7–11-in. (18–28 cm) piece of beading wire. String a round spacer, a crimp bead, a round spacer, and the jump ring. Go back through the beads just strung, tighten the wire, and crimp the crimp bead (Basics, p 12). Repeat.

3 On each end, string a flat spacer, a bicone crystal, a flat spacer, and an 8 mm round pearl. Repeat five times.

4 On each end, string a flat spacer, a bicone, and a flat spacer. String 6 mm round pearls until the strand is within 1 in. (2.5 cm) of the finished length.

5 On each end, string a round spacer, a crimp bead, a round spacer, and half of a toggle clasp. Go back through the beads just strung and tighten the wire. Check the fit, and add or remove beads if necessary. Crimp the crimp bead and trim the excess wire.

1 earrings • On a head pin, string: round spacer, bicone crystal, flat spacer, round pearl, flat spacer, bicone, round spacer. Make a wrapped loop (Basics, p. 12).

2 Open the loop of an earring wire (Basics, p. 12). Attach the dangle and close the loop. Make a second earring.

Supplies

necklace 18½ in. (47 cm)
- **12** 8 mm round pearls
- **8–14** 6 mm round pearls
- **14** 6 mm bicone crystals
- **28** 6 mm flat spacers
- **8** 3 mm round spacers
- 7½-in. (19.1 cm) iron-on appliqué
- flexible beading wire, .014 or .015
- **2** 6 mm jump rings
- **4** crimp beads
- toggle clasp
- **2** pairs of pliers (may include chainnose, roundnose, and/or bentnose)
- diagonal wire cutters
- micro-hole punch
- crimping pliers (optional)

earrings
- **2** 8 mm round pearls
- **4** 6 mm bicone crystals
- **4** 6 mm flat spacers
- **4** 3 mm round spacers
- **2** 2½-in. (6.4 cm) head pins
- pair of earring wires
- chainnose and roundnose pliers
- diagonal wire cutters

Design alternative

I used bead units to attach copper chain to this flower appliqué.

4 Cut two 4–5-in. (10–13 cm) pieces of copper chain. On one end of each, use a jump ring to attach an end loop of the beaded section.

1 necklace • Make the necklace units (p. 170). Open a jump ring (Basics, p. 12). Attach one loop of an amethyst-nugget unit, one hole of a copper washer, and one loop of an 8 mm crystal unit. Close the jump ring.

CONNECT

2 Use a jump ring to connect the other hole of the washer, the other loop of the crystal unit, and one loop of a triple-square unit.

Combine tones of copper, bronze, and lavender in a multitextured necklace and bracelet

by Kerri Fuhr

When I mixed these elements, I chose the lavender accents to add a pop of color. They pick up the iridescence in the pearls and the details in my handmade lampworked beads. Experiment with different beads — flat, rounded, jagged, smooth — and link them to your heart's content. There really are no rules — just follow your instincts!

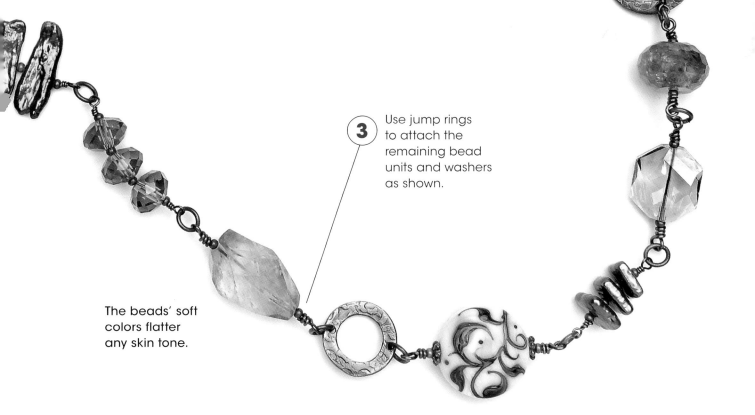

COPPERY
components

3 Use jump rings to attach the remaining bead units and washers as shown.

The beads' soft colors flatter any skin tone.

Necklace units

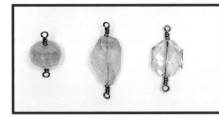

amethyst and 16 mm crystal units •
Cut a 3-in. (7.6 cm) piece of
22-gauge wire. Make a wrapped
loop (Basics, p. 12) on one end.
String a round spacer, an amethyst
rondelle, and a round spacer.
Make a wrapped loop. Make three
amethyst-rondelle units.

   Use 3½-in. (8.9 cm) pieces of
wire to make three amethyst-
nugget units and three 16 mm
crystal units.

8 mm crystal units • Use
2½-in. (6.4 cm) pieces of
24-gauge wire to make two
8 mm crystal units.

Tip
You can substitute
11° seed beads for
the round copper
spacers.

triple-bead units • Cut a 3-in.
(7.6 cm) piece of 24-gauge wire.
Make a wrapped loop on one
end. String four round spacers
alternated with three square pearls.
Make a wrapped loop. Make two
triple-square units. Use 4-in. (10 cm)
pieces of 24-gauge wire to make
two triple-stick-pearl units and a
triple-crystal-rondelle unit.

lampworked-bead units •
Cut a 3½-in. (8.9 cm) piece
of 22-gauge wire. Make a
wrapped loop on one end.
String: round spacer, flat
spacer, lampworked bead,
flat spacer, round spacer.
Make a wrapped loop.
Make three lampworked-
bead units.

Design alternative

In her "Ancient Treasures"
necklace, Kerri combined a
genuine ammonite fossil with
smoky quartz. She included
the bee bead because bees
were some of the earliest
insects to appear on the
earth, pollinating plants
80 million years ago!

Bracelet units

amethyst and 16 mm
crystal units • Follow
"Necklace units" to make
an amethyst-rondelle unit,
an amethyst-nugget unit,
and a 16 mm crystal unit.

crystal-rondelle units •
Use 2½-in. (6.4 cm) pieces
of 22-gauge wire to make
two crystal-rondelle units.

lampworked-bead unit •
Follow "Necklace units" to
make a lampworked-
bead unit.

pearl units • On a
head pin, string a round
pearl. Make a wrapped
loop (Basics, p. 12). Make
15 pearl units.

Supplies

necklace 35 in. (89 cm)
- **3** 22–25 mm faceted amethyst nuggets
- **6** 20–24 mm stick pearls
- **3** 20–22 mm lampworked beads
- **3** 16 mm flat crystals
- **3** 15–16 mm faceted amethyst rondelles
- **6** 10–11 mm square pearls, center drilled
- **3** 8–12 mm crystal rondelles
- **2** 8 mm flat or round crystals
- **6** 5 mm flat spacers
- **48** 2 mm round copper spacers
- **4** 16–20 mm patterned copper washers with two drilled holes
- 40½ in. (1 m) 22-gauge wire
- 23 in. (58 cm) 24-gauge wire

- 8–11 in. (20–28 cm) copper chain, 7–8 mm links
- **22** 5–6 mm jump rings
- lobster claw clasp
- chainnose and roundnose pliers
- diagonal wire cutters

bracelet
- 22–25 mm faceted amethyst nugget
- 20–22 mm lampworked bead
- 16 mm flat crystal
- 15–16 mm faceted amethyst rondelle
- **2** 8–12 mm crystal rondelles
- **15** 6–8 mm round pearls
- **2** 5 mm flat spacers
- **12** 2 mm round copper spacers

- **2** 16–20 mm patterned copper washers with two drilled holes
- 18½ in. (47 cm) 22-gauge wire
- 2 in. (5 cm) copper chain, 7–8 mm links
- **15** 1½-in. (3.8 cm) head pins
- **9** 5–6 mm jump rings
- lobster claw clasp
- chainnose and roundnose pliers
- diagonal wire cutters

Lampworked beads from Kerri Fuhr, kerrifuhr.com. Copper washers from Susan Lambert, susanlambert.etsy.com.

3 Use jump rings to attach the remaining bead units and washers as shown.

2 Use a jump ring to attach the other loop of the crystal-rondelle unit, three pearl units, and a hole of a copper washer.

1 bracelet • Make the bracelet units (p. 170). Open a jump ring (Basics, p. 12). Attach a lobster claw clasp and one loop of a crystal-rondelle unit. Close the jump ring.

4 Use a jump ring to attach the end loop of the last bead unit and a 2-in. (5 cm) piece of copper chain.

5 Use a jump ring to attach three pearl units and the end link of chain.

Tip
You can substitute Crystallized Swarovski Elements 12 mm or 18 mm graphic crystals (article #5520) for the 16 mm flat crystals.

Seeing STARS

Four fun projects for Fourth of July style

by Jane Konkel

My latest obsession? Stars. So when editor Cathy Jakicic brought home this garnet red and lapis blue gemstone chain from the Tucson Gem and Mineral Show, it was a sign to design a star-spangled something or other. Independence Day bonus: Premade chain makes for quick beading, leaving you free to set off a few fireworks of your own.

1 wood necklace • On a head pin, string an 11º seed bead and a hole of a star (Tip, previous page). Make the first half of a wrapped loop (Basics, p. 12). Make five star units.

2 Cut a 1½-in. (3.8 cm) and a 4½-in. (11.4 cm) piece of color A beaded chain. Cut a 3-in. (7.6 cm) and a 6-in. (15 cm) piece of color B beaded chain. Attach a star unit to one end of each chain and complete the wraps.

3 On a head pin, string an 11º and the remaining hole of the fifth star unit. Make the first half of a wrapped loop. Attach the remaining end of each chain and complete the wraps.

4 Cut two 8–10-in. (20 cm) pieces of color A chain and two 8–10-in. (20 cm) pieces of color B chain. Attach alternating colors of chain to the top star's loop and complete the wraps.

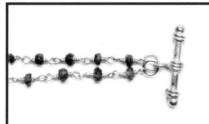

5 Open a jump ring (Basics, p. 12). Attach the end of a color A chain and half of a toggle clasp. Close the jump ring. Repeat with the end of a color B chain. Use jump rings to attach the remaining chains and clasp half.

Supplies

wood necklace 28 in. (71 cm)
- **5** 45 mm wood stars, with two holes
- **6** 11º seed beads
- **6** 1½-in. (3.8 cm) head pins
- 23–28 in. (58–71 cm) beaded chain, color A
- 26–30 in. (66–76 cm) beaded chain, color B
- **4** 4 mm jump rings
- toggle clasp
- chainnose and roundnose pliers
- diagonal wire cutters

wood earrrings
- **2** 45 mm wood stars
- **2** 11º seed beads
- **2** 1½-in. (3.8 cm) head pins
- 3½ in. (8.9 cm) beaded chain
- pair of earring wires
- chainnose and roundnose pliers
- diagonal wire cutters

brass necklace 17 in. (43 cm)
- **4** 32 mm brass stars, with loop
- 5 in. (13 cm) beaded chain, color A
- 13–17 in. (33–43 cm) beaded chain, color B
- **8** 4 mm jump rings
- toggle clasp
- **2** pairs of pliers
- diagonal wire cutters

brass earrings
- **2** 32 mm brass stars, with loop
- 3 in. (7.6 cm) beaded chain, color A
- **2** 4 mm jump rings
- pair of earring wires
- **2** pairs of pliers
- diagonal wire cutters

Wood star beads from Rings & Things, rings-things.com. Brass stars from Studio 500, studio500.etsy.com.

66Team the brass earrings with a wardrobe staple: a nautical striped top.**99**
—Jane

1 wood earrings • For each earring: Make a star unit as in step 1 of the wood necklace. Cut a 1½-in. (3.8 cm) piece of beaded chain. Attach the star unit's loop and one end of the chain. Complete the wraps.

2 Open the loop of an earring wire (Basics, p. 12). Attach the dangle and close the loop.

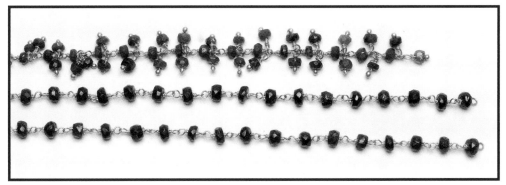

1 brass necklace • Cut a 5-in. (13 cm) piece of color A beaded chain, and two 6–8-in. (15–20 cm) pieces of color B chain.

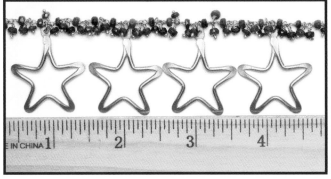

2 Open a jump ring (Basics, p. 12) and attach a star about 1 in. (2.5 cm) from one end of the color A chain. Close the jump ring. Use jump rings to attach the remaining stars about 1 in. (2.5 cm) apart.

3 Use jump rings to attach each end of the color A chain and one end of a color B chain. Check the fit and trim chain if necessary. Use jump rings to attach each end and half of a clasp.

1 brass earrings • For each earring: Cut a 1¼-in. (3.2 cm) piece of beaded chain. Open a jump ring (Basics, p. 12) and attach a star. Close the jump ring.

2 Open the loop of an earring wire and attach the dangle.

First time's a charm

A simple textured piece is the perfect way to try metal clay

by Irina Miech

In the metal clay classes I teach, there are always a few stringers who want to add some metal clay skills to their jewelry repertoire. This project is a great way to dip your toe in. Don't worry if you don't have a kiln; many bead stores (or art departments at local colleges) will fire your pieces for a nominal fee. There are also some very accessible no-kiln options on page 179.

8 Use a jump ring to attach a hook clasp to the other end.

7 Attach the head pin unit to the end link of the chain. Complete the wraps.

head pin unit • On a head pin, string a pearl. Make the first half of a wrapped loop (Basics, p. 12).

1 **necklace** • Make the head pin unit and bead units (right). Cut a 6-in. (15 cm), a 3-in. (7.6 cm), a 2-in. (5 cm), and two ½-in. (1.3 cm) pieces of chain.

bead unit • Cut a 3-in. (7.6 cm) piece of 24-gauge wire. Make the first half of a wrapped loop (Basics, p. 12). String a 9–12 mm bead and make the first half of a wrapped loop. Make three or four 9–12 mm bead units and six to eight rondelle units.

6 On the last loop, attach the 6-in. (15 cm) chain. Complete the wraps.

2 On one end of the 3-in. (7.6 cm) chain, attach: bead unit, ½-in. (1.3 cm) chain, bead unit, ½-in. (1.3 cm) chain, bead unit. Complete the wraps as you go, leaving the last loop open.

5 Attach the rondelle units, completing the wraps as you go. Leave the last loop open.

Make a second hole to turn the charm into a link, or make a multistrand wrap-around necklace. See page 179 for the design alternative.

3 On the last loop, attach the 2-in. (5 cm) chain and complete the wraps.

4 Open a jump ring (Basics, p. 12). Attach the charm and the center link of the 2-in. (5 cm) chain. Close the jump ring.

1 charm • Form about 6–8 g of clay into a ball. Apply a thin layer of balm to the clay.

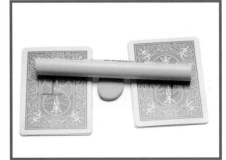

2 Apply a thin layer of balm to your roller and work surface. Stack four playing cards on each side of the clay and roll out the clay to the thickness of the card stacks.

3 With the roller, press the clay onto a texture sheet. Remove the clay and place a leaf vein side down on the untextured side. Stack three cards and imprint the leaf pattern with the roller.

4 Use a tissue blade or craft knife to cut out a leaf shape.

5 Let the charm dry completely. To curve the charm, drape it over a pen or pencil as it dries.

6 After the piece is dry, twist the tip of the knife to make a hole. Smooth the edges with a metal file.

7 Use a fine-grade sanding pad to smooth the edges. Fire your piece according to the manufacturer's directions (Firing tips, next page).

8 Burnish the fired piece with a polishing brush and soapy water to create a shiny surface. Finish with a polishing cloth if desired.

Tips

• Lump clay can dry out quickly. Keep unused portions in plastic wrap and mist with water to moisten the clay you're working with as needed.

• Your finished piece will be slightly smaller than when you put it in the kiln; PMC3 shrinks about 12% in volume when fired.

Design alternative

The patina on the metal clay charms was created by dipping them in a liver of sulfur (LOS) solution.

How-to: Dissolve about 1 tsp. of LOS crystals or gel and 1 tsp. of ammonia to very hot, but not boiling, water. Use tweezers to quickly dip the charms in the solution and then in clean, cold water. Dry the charm. Check the color and repeat until you achieve the desired effect. You can polish off areas of the patina with a polishing pad, brush, or cloth.

Firing tips

- If you're making a curved charm, fire it in a bowl of vermiculite so the piece doesn't flatten on the floor of the kiln.
- A kiln — even a small one — is an investment. Kiln-firing is usually the best option so, if possible, bring your piece to a local bead store to fire for a small fee. Check with the store for restrictions on firing.

Torch firing

Torch firing is an option for this project because PMC3 is a low-firing clay. Use a butane torch — like you'd use with crème brûlée — and a firing brick. Place the unfired metal clay piece in the middle of a firing brick. Dim the lights and hold the torch at a 45° angle 2 in. (5 cm) from the piece. You will see a small amount of smoke and flame, and then the piece will turn white. Keep the torch moving over the piece until you see the piece glow. When the piece turns a peach color, begin timing the firing. Firing time ranges from 1 to 5 minutes, depending on weight. The charm in this project uses about 8 grams of clay so it should take about 90 seconds. When finished, use tweezers to move your piece to the cooler edge of the firing brick and allow it to cool.

Metal clay pieces must be under 25 grams in weight and no larger than a United States silver dollar to be torch fired. You cannot torch fire pieces if the main component is sheet or paper clay or if the piece is formed around cork clay. Torch firing with cork clay can create open flames and is hazardous. Check out more information on torch firing as well as stove-top firing at ArtJewelryMag.com.

Supplies

necklace 17 in. (43 cm)

- PMC3 clay (one package)
- **3-4** 9–12 mm beads
- 6–8 mm potato pearl
- **6-8** 6 mm rondelles
- 27–36 in. (69–90 cm) 24-gauge half-hard wire
- 12 in. (30 cm) chain, 4–5 mm links
- 1½-in. (3.8 cm) head pin
- **2** 7 mm jump rings
- hook clasp
- chainnose and roundnose pliers
- diagonal wire cutters
- acrylic roller
- burnishing brush
- craft knife or tissue blade
- fine-grade sanding pad
- kiln or torch for firing
- metal file
- natural lip balm or other release medium
- **8** playing cards
- texture sheet and leaf
- tweezers
- pen or pencil (optional)
- polishing cloth (optional)

Combine Bali silver tubes, Lucite disks from Germany, and clay whorl beads from Africa, and you've got global appeal. (What are whorl beads? They're the asymmetrical bicones shaped like spindle whorls for spinning thread or yarn.) The dots, stripes, and geometric patterns come together in one incredible necklace.

String a striking necklace with bold silver tubes

by Rupa Balachandar

Exotic curves

1 necklace • Cut a piece of beading wire (Basics, p. 12). Center a spacer, a 30 mm whorl bead, and a spacer. On each end, string: 28–30 mm disk bead, 18–20 mm disk bead, spacer, 15–20 mm accent bead, spacer, 15–20 mm whorl bead, spacer.

2 Detach the end caps from two tube beads for easier stringing. On each end of the strand, string an end cap, a tube, and an end cap. Tighten the end caps on the tubes.

3 On each end, string spacers until the strand is within 2 in. (5 cm) of the finished length. Check the fit, and add or remove beads if necessary. Add half of a clasp (Basics, p. 13).

Supplies

necklace 18½ in. (47 cm)
- **2** 4½-in. (11.4 cm) curved silver tube beads with detachable end caps
- 30 mm clay whorl bead
- **2** 28–30 mm Lucite disk beads
- **2** 18–20 mm Lucite disk beads
- **2** 15–20 mm clay whorl beads
- **2** 15–20 mm silver accent beads
- **12–18** 6 mm round spacers
- flexible beading wire, .018 or .019
- **2** crimp beads
- ½ in. (1.3 cm) French (bullion) wire
- hook-and-eye clasp
- chainnose or crimping pliers
- diagonal wire cutters

earrings
- **2** 16 mm silver accent beads
- **2** 6 mm round fire-polished crystals
- **2** 5–6 mm bicone beads
- **2** 2-in. (5 cm) head pins
- pair of lever-back earring wires
- chainnose and roundnose pliers
- diagonal wire cutters

Tip

When finishing the necklace, you can substitute a Wire Guardian for the French wire on each end.

1 earrings • On a head pin, string a round crystal, an accent bead, and a bicone bead. Make a wrapped loop (Basics, p. 12).

2 Open the loop of an earring wire (Basics, p 12). Attach the dangle and close the loop. Make a second earring.

Design alternative

If you prefer a more subdued style, string a necklace in the same palette with scaled-down materials.

66 I love to travel, and I really can't say I have a favorite place. But I seem to have a preference for island locales. **99** –Rupa

LAYERED
polymer pendants

Clay makes a cameo appearance

by Jill Erickson

I found these 1960s Thingmaker "Creepy Crawler" and "Fun Flower" molds on eBay, but this nontraditional take on cameos can be made from cookie stamps, candy or soap molds, or any pendant-size mold you have around. To maintain the traditional palette of this historical mourning jewelry, use the lighter color for the image and the darker for the base.

Pendant

1 Spritz a mold with water. Knead the light-colored clay with your hands until it is malleable. Roll a piece between your hands to make a ball. Press the ball into the mold.

2 Use a tissue blade to scrape the excess clay from the mold, leaving only the depression filled with clay.

3 Knead the dark clay until it is malleable. Roll it into a ball and use an acrylic roller to flatten it to ¼ in. (6 mm) thick.

4 Place the dark clay over the light clay in the mold. Using moderate pressure, roll the acrylic roller over the clay. Carefully peel the dark clay off the mold. The light clay should be attached to the dark clay.

5 Place the clay on your work surface with the molded portion facing up. Use a shape cutter or the tissue blade to trim the excess dark clay. Use a needle to make a hole centered at the top. Place the clay on a ceramic tile and bake it according to the manufacturer's instructions.

4 On each end, over both wires, string two 4 mm pearls, a crimp bead, and half of a toggle clasp. Check the fit and add or remove beads if necessary. Go back through the beads just strung and tighten the wires. Crimp the crimp bead (Basics, p. 13) and trim the excess wire.

3 On each end, string six 11⁰s and the next 6 mm pearl. Tighten the wire to curve each set of 11⁰s. Repeat until you've strung the last 6 mm pearl.

"I really enjoy being part of the students' journey as a new skill becomes a gateway to making their work more personal." —Jill

Cut a 37–42-in. (.9–1.1 m) piece of beading wire. Center six 11⁰ seed beads. On each end, string the wire through the 6 mm pearl next to the center pearl.

2

1 necklace • Make the pendant (previous page). Cut a piece of beading wire (Basics, p. 12). Center a 4 mm pearl. On each end, string an alternating pattern of 6 mm and 4 mm pearls until the strand is the desired length.

5 Open a jump ring (Basics, p. 12). Attach the pendant over the center beads. Close the jump ring.

Design alternative

In this version, I sandwiched two pieces of dark clay together to create a channel for a bezel of strung pearls and clay. Instead of drilling a hole for a jump ring, I strung the pearls and embedded a piece of flexible beading wire in the bezel layer before I baked the pendant.

Editor's note

If you're a fan of the Thingmaker molds, we found a source for them at austinthompson.org/thingmaker/main.shtm.

Supplies

pendant
- 1 oz. package polymer clay, light color
- 1 oz. package polymer clay, dark color
- acrylic roller
- mold
- needle
- shape cutter
- small ceramic tile
- spritz bottle of water
- tissue blade
- toaster oven dedicated to craft use
- packing or painter's tape (optional)

necklace 18 in. (46 cm)
- **44–48** 6 mm glass pearls
- **46–50** 4 mm glass pearls
- 1 g 11º seed beads
- flexible beading wire, .010 or .011
- 9 mm jump ring
- **2** crimp beads
- toggle clasp
- chainnose and roundnose pliers, or **2** pairs of chainnose pliers
- crimping pliers (optional)

Tips

- Polymer clay is available at craft stores.
- Kneading the clay not only makes it easier to work with but also helps it to bake properly.
- If you're using a mold with more than one depression, tape the unused areas so the darker clay will roll more smoothly. The tape will stick better if you apply it before you spritz the mold with water.
- Put aluminum foil over the clay when baking to protect the lighter color from darkening.
- Preheat the oven for a more consistent temperature.

Tiny treasure earrings

Use resin to turn precious bits into keepsake earrings

by Lori Mendenhall

Handmade earring wires add an artisanal look to resin-filled bezels.

I love filling polymer clay bezels with pearls, charms, dried flowers, dichroic films, fibers, and glitter. Locking all of the elements down with resin gave me the freedom to work with almost anything I wanted. So I experimented with pre-made metal bezels; I love their shiny finish and smooth lines. They're a great way to preserve your favorite gemstones.

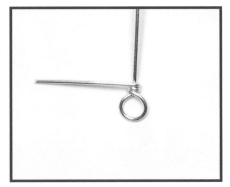

1 For each earring, fill a bezel with gemstone chips (Chip tips, next page).

Wearing safety goggles and gloves, pour equal parts resin and hardener into a plastic cup. Using a craft stick, stir slowly and gently for two minutes, scraping down the sides of the cup. Pour the mixture into a clean cup and stir with a clean craft stick for one minute.

2 Using the craft stick, drip the mixture into each bezel. Use a heat gun or gently exhale on the bezel to release bubbles from the mixture. Cover the bezels with a box and allow to cure.

3 For each earring wire: Cut a 4-in. (10 cm) piece of wire. In the center of the wire, using the largest part of your roundnose pliers, make a wrapped loop (Basics, p. 12). Do not trim the excess wire.

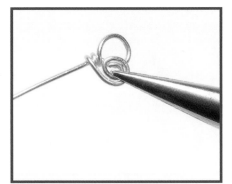

4 Use roundnose pliers to make a small loop on the end of the wire tail. Grasping the loop with chainnose pliers, continue coiling the wire until you reach the wraps. Use chainnose pliers to position the coil next to the wrapped loop.

5 String a 6–7 mm bead. Above the bead, make a right-angle bend perpendicular to the wrapped loop. Pull the wire around the barrel of a pen.

Design alternative

You can also add elements like wire coils, flat-back crystals, and angular earring wires. Just make sure you don't get any resin on the crystals (otherwise the sparkle will be muted).

Chip tips

- Experiment with different quantities of chips to achieve a look you like. The turquoise earrings have a smooth, flat layer of resin covering them, creating a glassy look. The green chrysoprase chips are larger and extend above the rim of the bezel, giving a more sculptural appearance.
- Choose chips in various sizes, shapes, and with different marks and veining. The contrast will produce great results.
- Pouring resin over gemstones may change their color slightly. For example, the rose quartz chips I used look more peach than pink.

before

after

Supplies

- **2** 6–7 mm beads
- **14–50** 2–8 mm gemstone chips
- **2** 15–25 mm bezels with loops
- 8 in. (20 cm) 20-gauge half-hard wire
- **2** 4 mm jump rings
- EasyCast Clear Casting Epoxy
- mixing cups
- plastic gloves
- safety goggles
- wooden craft sticks
- chainnose and roundnose pliers
- diagonal wire cutters
- hammer
- bench block or anvil
- metal file or emery board
- pen
- box (to cover pieces while they cure)
- heat gun (optional)

6 Use pliers to curve the end of the wire up. Trim the excess wire and file the end if necessary.

7 On a bench block or anvil, gently hammer the earring wire. Hammer the other side.

8 Open a jump ring (Basics, p 12). Attach the loop of the bezel and the loop of the earring wire. Close the jump ring.

❝I achieved the look of a bezel-set stone in a different and unexpected way.❞
—Lori

Wear winter

A handmade metal clay bead accents pastels

by Cathy Jakicic

The coolness of a hollow metal clay lentil bead creates a beautiful contrast to the subtle warmth of the whites and soft lavenders in this project.

Tip

Plan out the patterns on a bead board before you begin stringing. It will make bead placement easier and let you judge the strand lengths more accurately.

Supplies

necklace 21–25 in. (53–64 cm)

- 25 mm hollow metal clay lentil bead
- **2** 16-in. (41 cm) strands 25 mm quartz nuggets
- **2** 16-in. (41 cm) strands 15 mm carved quartz rose beads
- 16-in. (41 cm) strand 15 mm kunzite chips
- **12–14** 12 mm silver saucer beads
- **8–10** 12 mm crystal rondelles
- **2** 8-in. (20 cm) strands 10 mm quartz rondelles
- **10–12** 8 mm crystal rondelles
- 16-in. (41 cm) strand 6–8 mm quartz round beads
- flexible beading wire, .018 or .019
- **6** crimp beads
- **6** crimp covers
- three-strand box clasp
- chainnose or crimping pliers
- diagonal wire cutters

earrings

- **2** 15 mm carved quartz rose beads
- **2** 8 mm crystal rondelles
- **4** 4 mm flat spacers
- **2** 2-in. (5 cm) head pins
- pair of earring wires
- chainnose and roundnose pliers
- diagonal wire cutters

whites

1

necklace

1 Cut a piece of beading wire (Basics, p. 12) for the longest strand. String a metal clay bead. On one end, string 9–10 in. (23–25 cm) of nuggets, chips, rose beads, and round beads. On the other end, string 13–15 in. (33–38 cm) of beads.

2 For the middle strand: Cut a piece of beading wire 2 in. (5 cm) shorter than the first. String quartz and crystal rondelles interspersed with saucer beads and rounds until the strand is within 1 in. (2.5 cm) of the finished length.

3 For the shortest strand: Cut a piece of beading wire 2 in. (5 cm) shorter than the second. String nuggets, chips, roses, rondelles, and saucers until the strand is within 1 in. (2.5 cm) of the finished length.

The silver focal bead will be a reference for the placement of the silver beads in the two shorter strands.

1 On each end of each strand, string a round bead, a crimp bead, a round, and the corresponding loop of half of a box clasp. Go back through the last beads strung and tighten the wire. Crimp the crimp bead (Basics, p. 13) and trim the excess wire.

2 Using chainnose or crimping pliers, gently close a crimp cover over each crimp.

"Silver against a varied palette of whites has a beautiful fairy-tale quality." —Cathy

Design alternative

- Flip the necklace around so the cameo clasp is in front.
- Replace the metal clay bead with a Venetian glass saucer to add a splash of color.

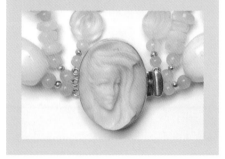

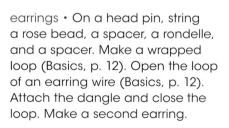

earrings • On a head pin, string a rose bead, a spacer, a rondelle, and a spacer. Make a wrapped loop (Basics, p. 12). Open the loop of an earring wire (Basics, p. 12). Attach the dangle and close the loop. Make a second earring.

Potluck challenge

Five staffers work from a collection of beads

The staff of *Bead Style* looks forward to shopping at each Bead&Button Show, so we decided to craft a challenge around it. Each staff member bought five of a different material: large beads, small beads, accent beads, a focal piece, and chain (plus the copper flowers as a wild card). There was some trading of elements as the designing began, and not everybody used everything.

Potluck elements

- 25–30 mm filigree bead
- 16-in. (41 cm) strand 7–15 mm graduated rainbow soocho jade rondelles
- **10** 7–13 mm metallic Lucite nuggets
- 16-in. (41 cm) strand 5–12 mm pearls, top drilled
- 40 mm three-petal flower component
- 24 in. (61 cm) chain, 6–8 mm links

"Kitchen sink" necklace shows that more can sometimes be more

by Cathy Jakicic

1 necklace • Cut a 13–14-in. (33–36 cm) piece of beading wire. String 6½–7½ in. (16.5–19.1 cm) of rondelles interspersed with pearls and metallic nuggets. On each end, string a crimp bead and a soldered jump ring. Go back through the last few beads strung and tighten the wire. Crimp the crimp bead (Basics, p. 12) and trim the excess wire.

> **❝I couldn't decide between the flowers and the filigrees for the focal piece so I naturally bought both.❞**
> —Cathy

2 Cut a 12–13-in. (30–33 cm) piece of beading wire. String 5½–6½ in. (14–16.5 cm) of beads, including the filigree bead near one end. Finish the strand as in step 1.

3 Cut a 10-in. (25 cm) piece of beading wire. String 4 in. (10 cm) of pearls.

Tips

- On the pearl strands, string at least one larger pearl on each end. This will make it easier to bring the beading wire back through before crimping the crimp beads.
- For a balanced composition, position the copper flower across from the rondelle strand with the filigree bead.

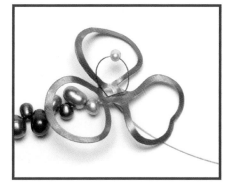

4 Cut a 12-in. (30 cm) piece of beading wire. String 1½ in. (3.8 cm) of pearls. Bring the wire up through the center of the flower component. String a pearl and go back through the flower's center. Tighten the wire. String pearls until the strand is 6 in. (13 cm) long.

5 On one end of each pearl strand, string a crimp bead and the jump ring closest to the filigree of the short rondelle strand. Go back through the last few beads strung and tighten the wire. Crimp the crimp bead and trim the excess wire. Attach the remaining ends of the pearl strands and the jump ring of the other rondelle strand.

6 Cut a 5½-in. (14 cm) piece of chain. Open a jump ring (Basics, p. 12) and attach the chain between the pearl strands to one of the soldered jump rings. Close the jump ring. Repeat with the other end of the chain.

7 Cut a 16½–18-in. (41.9–46 cm) piece of chain. Use a jump ring to attach one end of the chain, half of a clasp, and the soldered jump ring on the end of a rondelle strand. Repeat on the other end of the chain.

1 earrings • On an eye pin, string a nugget and a rondelle. Make a plain loop (Basics, p. 12).

2 Cut a three-link and a four-link piece of chain. Open a loop (Basics, p. 12) of the bead unit and attach the chains. Close the loop. Open the loop of the earring wire. Attach the dangle and close the loop. Make a second earring.

Supplies

necklace 18 in. (46 cm)
- ◆ potluck elements
- ◆ flexible beading wire, .012
- ◆ **4** 7 mm soldered jump rings
- ◆ **2** 7 mm jump rings
- ◆ **8** crimp beads
- ◆ toggle clasp
- ◆ chainnose and roundnose pliers
- ◆ diagonal wire cutters

earrings
- ◆ potluck elements
- ◆ **2** 2-in. (5 cm) eye pins
- ◆ **8** crimp beads
- ◆ pair of earring wires
- ◆ chainnose and roundnose pliers
- ◆ diagonal wire cutters

Play up individual materials in a simple necklace and bracelet

by Naomi Fujimoto

Tip

When using 23 mm jump rings in the necklace, string metallic nuggets with larger holes.

1 necklace • Cut a 7-in. (18 cm) piece of wire. String a 10–12 mm pearl and the center of a metal flower. Twist the wire end and the stem together. Trim the excess wire.

2 Wrap the wire around the base of a petal four or five times.

3 Bring the wire behind the flower and wrap the wire around the base of two petals across from the first set of wraps. Trim the excess wire and tuck the ends.

4 On a bench block or anvil, hammer a 23 mm jump ring. Hammer the other side. Make six hammered jump rings.

5 Open a hammered jump ring (Basics, p. 12). Attach a nugget and close the jump ring.

6 Decide how long you want your necklace to be and cut a piece of chain to that length. Use a 14 mm jump ring to attach the flower and the center link of chain.

7 On each side, about 1–1½ in. (2.5–3.8 cm) from the center, use a 14 mm jump ring to attach a nugget unit. Attach the remaining nugget units.

8 Check the fit, and trim chain if necessary. On one end, use a 4–5 mm jump ring to attach a lobster claw clasp. Repeat on the other end, substituting a 14 mm jump ring for the clasp.

9 On a head pin, string three 5–12 mm pearls. Make the first half of a wrapped loop (Basics, p. 12). Attach the jump ring on the end of the necklace and complete the wraps.

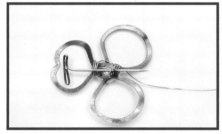

1 bracelet • Cut a 7-in. (18 cm) piece of wire. Attach a pearl to the center of a flower as in steps 1 to 3 of the necklace, wrapping the wire around a T-pin or embroidery needle in back of the flower. Remove the needle.

2 Measure your wrist, add 6 in. (15 cm), and cut a piece of ribbon elastic to that length. String a twisted-wire needle. String pearls until the strand is within ½ in. (1.3 cm) of the finished length.

3 String the metal flower. Tie a surgeon's knot (Basics, p. 12) and apply glue to the knot. Trim the excess elastic to ⅛ in. (3 mm). Stretch the bracelet gently to slide the knot under the wire wraps.

Supplies

necklace 17 in. (43 cm)
- potluck elements
- 10–12 mm pearl
- 7 in. (18 cm) 24- or 26-gauge wire
- 1½-in. (3.8 cm) head pin
- **6** 23 mm jump rings
- **8** 14 mm jump rings
- **2** 4–5 mm jump rings
- lobster claw clasp
- chainnose and roundnose pliers
- diagonal wire cutters
- hammer
- anvil or bench block

bracelet
- potluck elements
- 10–12 mm pearl
- ribbon elastic
- 7 in. (18 cm) 24- or 26-gauge wire
- diagonal wire cutters
- scissors
- G-S Hypo Cement
- T-pin or embroidery needle
- twisted-wire needle

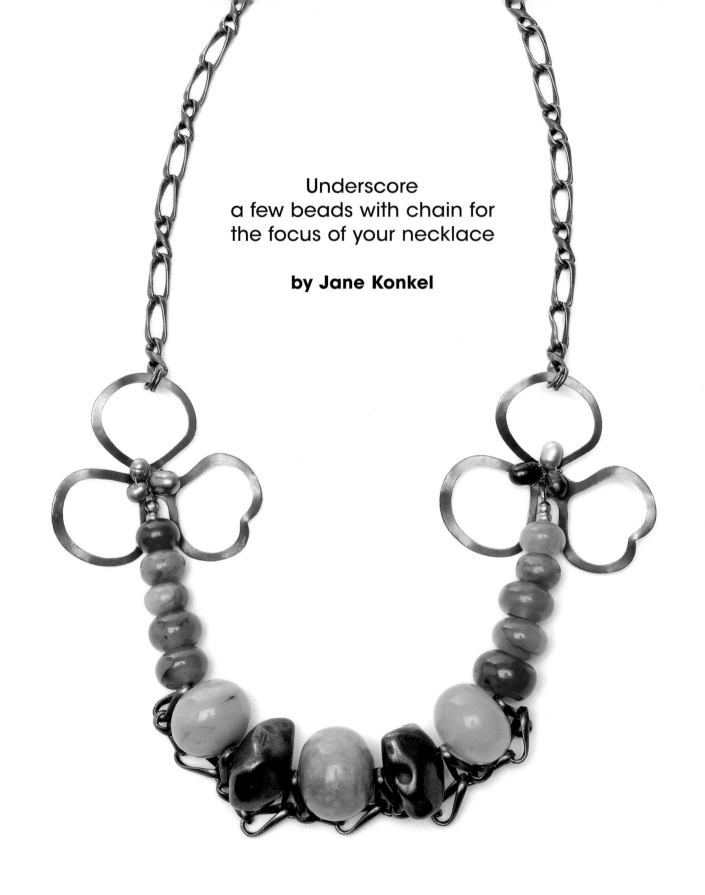

Underscore
a few beads with chain for
the focus of your necklace

by Jane Konkel

1 necklace • Cut a 6-in. (15 cm) piece of 26-gauge wire. Center three pearls on the wire. Over both ends, string a flower.

Wrap the ends a few times around the petals. Trim the excess wire and tuck the end. Make a second flower.

2 Cut two 4–7-in. (10–18 cm) pieces and one 8-in. (20 cm) piece of chain. Cut a 10-in. (25 cm) piece of beading wire. On one end of the beading wire, string a Wire Guardian and a flower.

3 String a spacer, a crimp bead, five rondelles (in ascending size), the end link of the 8-in. (20 cm) chain, a rondelle, and a link.

4 String: nugget, link, largest rondelle, link, nugget, link, rondelle, link. Trim the excess chain. String five rondelles (in descending size).

5 String a crimp bead, a spacer, a Wire Guardian, and the remaining flower. Go back through the beads just strung and tighten the wire. Crimp the crimp beads (Basics, p. 12). Close a crimp cover over each crimp bead.

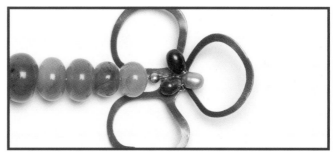

6 On each end, open a 4 mm jump ring (Basics p. 12) and attach a flower petal and a 4–7-in. (10–18 cm) chain. Close the jump ring. Attach another jump ring.

7 On one end, use a jump ring to attach a lobster claw clasp.

8 On a head pin, string a small rondelle and make the first half of a wrapped loop (Basics, p. 12). Attach the remaining chain and complete the wraps.

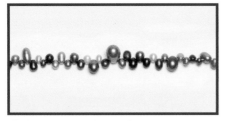

1 bracelet • Cut a 24-in. (61 cm) piece of 26-gauge wire. String 8 in. (20 cm) of pearls on the wire. Center the pearls.

2 String a loop of the bangle and wrap one end of the wire two or three times around the bangle. Slide a pearl next to the bangle and wrap the wire two or three times around the bangle.

3 Continue sliding pearls and wrapping the wire, stringing the wire through the loops as you go, until you reach the first loop. (Use additional pieces of 26-gauge wire as necessary.)

4 String the loop and wrap the end of the wire two or three times around the bangle. Trim the excess wire and tuck the ends.

Supplies

necklace 20 in. (51 cm)
- ◆ potluck elements
- ◆ flexible beading wire, .018 or .019
- ◆ 12 in. (30 cm) 26-gauge wire
- ◆ 2-in. (5 cm) head pin
- ◆ **5** 4 mm jump rings
- ◆ **2** crimp beads
- ◆ **2** crimp covers
- ◆ **2** Wire Guardians
- ◆ lobster claw clasp
- ◆ chainnose and roundnose pliers
- ◆ diagonal wire cutters
- ◆ crimping pliers (optional)

bracelet
- ◆ potluck elements
- ◆ bangle bracelet with loops
- ◆ 2 yd. (1.8 m) 26-gauge wire
- ◆ diagonal wire cutters

Tips

- For necklace chain that drapes, cut a longer piece in step 2.
- Because of the position of the flowers, crimping may be a challenge. If some wire shows on the ends, close crimp covers over the gaps.

66 I bought several styles of brass chain for the challenge. It was interesting to see which type Kelsey, Stacy, Cathy, and Naomi chose. 99 —Jane

One 16-in. (41 cm) strand of pearls is enough to make two bracelets.

Pick the prettiest palette for a rose-tinted set

by Kelsey Lawler

❝I picked out metallic resin nuggets for this challenge, but fell in love with what the other editors brought to the table. What can I say? Color calls to me.❞ —Kelsey

1 necklace • On a head pin, string a rondelle and make a wrapped loop (Basics, p. 12). Make 12 rondelle units.

2 Cut a piece of beading wire (Basics, p. 13). String a rondelle, a pearl, a rondelle unit, and a pearl. Repeat 11 times. String a rondelle and center the beads.

3 On each end, string pearls until the necklace is within 1 in. (2.5 cm) of the finished length. On one end, string a spacer, a crimp bead, a spacer, and a lobster claw clasp. Repeat on the other end, substituting a 3-in. (7.6 cm) piece of chain for the clasp. Check the fit, and add or remove beads if necessary. Go back through the beads just strung and tighten the wire. Crimp the crimp bead (Basics, p. 12); trim the excess wire.

Supplies

necklace 18 in. (46 cm)
- ◆ potluck elements
- ◆ **4** 4 mm spacers
- ◆ flexible beading wire, .018 or .019
- ◆ **12** 2-in. (5 cm) head pins
- ◆ **2** crimp beads
- ◆ lobster claw clasp
- ◆ chainnose and roundnose pliers
- ◆ diagonal wire cutters
- ◆ crimping pliers (optional)

bracelet
- ◆ potluck elements
- ◆ **4** 4 mm spacers
- ◆ flexible beading wire, .018 or .019
- ◆ **14–16** 2-in. (5 cm) head pins
- ◆ **2** crimp beads
- ◆ lobster claw clasp
- ◆ chainnose and roundnose pliers
- ◆ diagonal wire cutters
- ◆ crimping pliers (optional)

Tip

Arrange the rondelles and rondelle units before stringing to achieve a pleasing balance in size and color.

1 bracelet • On a head pin, string a rondelle and make a wrapped loop (Basics, p. 12). Make 14 to 16 rondelle units.

2 String a pearl, the two largest rondelle units, and a pearl. Center the beads.

On each end, string a rondelle, a pearl, the two next largest rondelle units, and a pearl. Repeat until the bracelet is within 1 in. (2.5 cm) of the finished length.

3 On one end, string a spacer, a crimp bead, a spacer, and a lobster claw clasp. Repeat on the other end, substituting a 1-in. (2.5 cm) piece of chain for the clasp. Finish as in step 3 of the necklace.

Confession: Kelsey "borrowed" some of her rosier rondelles from Naomi.

Two unusual pieces make for interchangeable pendants

by Stacy Werkheiser

"My contribution to the challenge was the soocho jade. I love the variety of berry-licious shades in these rondelles." —Stacy

1 box pendant • Cut a 5½-in. (14 cm) piece of 22-gauge wire. String the filigree bead. Make a set of wraps above the bead (Basics, p. 12). String a spacer, a 10–12 mm rondelle, and a spacer. Make a wrapped loop (Basics, p. 12).

2 Cut an 8-in. (20 cm) piece of wire and string the filigree bead. Make a set of wraps below the bead. String the largest rondelle, bring the wire around it, and wrap the wire around the previous wraps.

Supplies

1 flower pendant · Cut a 24-in. (61 cm) piece of 26-gauge wire. Wrap the wire four or five times around the flower at the base of a petal.

all projects
- potluck elements
- chainnose and roundnose pliers
- diagonal wire cutters

box pendant
- **2** 4 mm flat spacers
- 13½ in. (34.3 cm) 22-gauge wire

flower pendant
- 4 mm flat spacer
- 8 in. (20 cm) 22-gauge wire
- 2 yd. (1.8 m) 26-gauge wire

necklace 21–22 in. (53–56 cm)
- **30** 4 mm flat spacers
- flexible beading wire, .018 or .019
- 14 mm figure-8 connector
- 2-in. (5 cm) head pin
- 7–8 mm jump ring
- **4** crimp beads
- 17–18 mm lobster claw clasp
- crimping pliers (optional)

2 Wrap the wire two to five times around the petal. String a pearl and position it on top of the petal. Repeat until you've covered the petal. To end the wire, wrap two to five times around the petal. Trim the excess wire on the back of the flower and use chainnose pliers to tuck the end.

3 Repeat steps 1 and 2 for the remaining petals.

4 Cut an 8-in. (20 cm) piece of 22-gauge wire. On one end, make a small plain loop (Basics, p. 12). String a spacer, an 8–10 mm rondelle, and the center of the flower. Wrap once around each petal base. Bend the wire up behind the flower between two petals.

5 Make a wrapped loop (Basics, p. 12), making sure the wire clears the petals. Wrap all the way down the stem of the wire.

1 **necklace** • Open one loop of a figure-8 connector and attach a pendant. Close the loop. Cut a piece of beading wire (Basics, p. 13) and center the pendant. On each end, string five metallic nuggets.

2 **a** On each end, starting with the largest rondelles, string a rondelle and two spacers.

b On each end, string two rondelles, two spacers, three rondelles, and two spacers. Repeat the pattern twice. End with a rondelle, a crimp bead, a rondelle, and a crimp bead.

3 Cut a 23–24-in. (58–61 cm) piece of chain. On one end of the beaded strand, string the third link of chain. Go back through the last four beads strung and tighten the wire. Crimp the crimp beads (Basics, p. 13). Trim the excess wire.

4 On the other end of the beaded strand, string a link 4½–5 in. (11.4–13 cm) from the end of the chain. Go back through the last four beads strung and tighten the wire. Crimp the crimp beads and trim the excess wire.

5 Open a jump ring (Basics, p. 12) and attach the short end of the chain and a lobster claw clasp. Close the jump ring.

6 On a head pin, string a spacer, a rondelle, a spacer, and a rondelle. Make the first half of a wrapped loop.

7 Attach the dangle to the end of the chain. Complete the wraps.

Tips

- Place your strand of rondelles in the channel of a bead board before removing the original stringing material. This will keep the beads in their graduated order.
- Remove any inconsistently shaped rondelles in pairs before stringing so that the sides of your necklace are equal in length. Use these rondelles in the pendants.
- Use heavy-duty wire cutters to cut thick chain, or use two pairs of pliers to open a link where desired.

Glass &

Ceramic

Fabulous FAKES

Turn frugal into fun with an easy jewelry set ◆ by Naomi Fujimoto

Large crystals can get a bit heavy — as well as a bit pricey. But you can make a crystal-like necklace with vintage baubles you may already have on hand. I loved these graduated lavender necklaces and wanted to pair them with faceted glass drops, which came from a beaded curtain. Try a chandelier store for alternatives, or pair thrift-store beads with budget-friendly acrylic rounds in bright colors.

Supplies

drop necklace 15½ in. (39.4 cm)
- **5** 35–45 mm faceted glass drops
- 16-in. (41 cm) graduated bead necklace
- **30-36** 4 mm bicone crystals
- flexible beading wire, .014 or .015
- 35 in. (89 cm) 22- or 24-gauge half-hard wire
- 3 in. (7.6 cm) chain, 10–12 mm links
- 2-in. (5 cm) head pin
- **2** crimp beads
- lobster claw clasp
- chainnose and roundnose pliers
- diagonal wire cutters
- crimping pliers (optional)

purple-and-lavender necklace 16 in. (41 cm)
- 16-in. (41 cm) graduated bead necklace
- **5** 20 mm round acrylic beads
- **4-6** 15 mm round acrylic beads
- **5-7** 12 mm round acrylic beads
- **25-29** 4 mm bicone crystals
- 3 in. (7.6 cm) chain, 10–12 mm links
- 2-in. (5 cm) head pin
- **2** crimp beads
- lobster claw clasp
- chainnose and roundnose pliers
- diagonal wire cutters
- crimping pliers (optional)

Drop units

1 Cut a 7-in. (18 cm) piece of 22- or 24-gauge wire. String a glass drop and make a set of wraps above it (Basics, p. 12).

2 String a bicone crystal and make a wrapped loop (Basics, p. 12) perpendicular to the drop.

Attach a clasp and a chain extender (Finishing the necklace, p. 208).

4

3 On each end, string the remaining graduated beads in descending size, with a bicone between each, until the strand is within 1 in. (2.5 cm) of the finished length. End with a bicone.

2 On a beading board, remove the string from a graduated necklace. Remove the center bead. On each end, string: the next largest bead, drop unit, bicone, the next largest bead, drop unit, bicone.

1

drop necklace • Make five drop units (Drop units, previous page). Cut a piece of beading wire (Basics, p. 13). On the wire, center a bicone crystal, a drop unit, and a bicone.

Finishing the necklace

1 On one end, string a crimp bead, a bicone crystal, and a lobster claw clasp to add a clasp (Basics, p. 13). Repeat on the other end, substituting a 3-in. (7.6 cm) piece of chain for the clasp.

2 On a head pin, string a bicone and a round bead. Make the first half of a wrapped loop (Basics, p. 12). Attach the end link of chain and complete the wraps.

3 Attach a clasp and a chain extender (Finishing a necklace, above).

2 On each end, string graduated and round acrylic beads in descending size, with a bicone between each. End with a bicone.

1 purple-and-lavender necklace • On a beading board, remove the string from a graduated necklace. Remove the center bead. Cut a piece of beading wire (Basics, p. 13). On the wire, center a bicone crystal, a 20 mm round bead, and a bicone.

By mixing up the charms, no two bracelets will be exactly alike.

Create a
charming mix

Connect a variety of hearts in a sweet bracelet and earrings

by Alyce Shepardson

Hearts aren't just for Valentine's Day; you'll love this collection any time of year. Just mix glass and metal, puffy and hollow components, simple and ornate styles. For a pleasing effect, join contrasting pairs together on each jump ring. The contrast will make each of the charms pop.

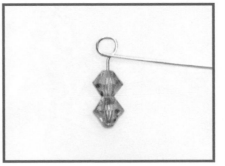

1 **bracelet** • Cut a 3-in. (7.6 cm) piece of wire. Make the first half of a wrapped loop (Basics, p. 12). String a heart bead and make the first half of a wrapped loop. Make six heart units.

2 On a head pin, string two bicone crystals. Make the first half of a wrapped loop. Make three crystal units.

3 Attach a soldered jump ring to each loop of a heart unit. Complete the wraps. On each end, attach a heart unit and a soldered jump ring. Continue attaching the remaining heart units and soldered jump rings, completing the wraps as you go.

4 Open a 4 mm jump ring (Basics, p. 12). Attach a heart charm and a soldered jump ring. Close the jump ring. Use another 4 mm jump ring to attach a second charm. Attach a pair of charms to each remaining soldered jump ring. Attach a crystal unit to every other soldered jump ring.

5 Cut a 6-in. (15 cm) piece of beading wire. Center a soldered jump ring from one end of the bracelet. Over both ends of the wire, string: round crystal, flat spacer, round crystal, crimp bead, half of a toggle clasp. Go back through the crimp bead and tighten the wire. Crimp the crimp bead (Basics, p. 13) and trim the excess wire. Repeat on the other side.

6 Close a crimp cover over each crimp.

Tips

- To lengthen or shorten the bracelet, adjust the size or number of crystals in step 5.
- When making heart units for the earrings, it's easier to make the wrapped loop first, then the plain loop. (Sometimes it's a challenge to make the wraps at the top of the heart bead and trim the wire close to the stem.)

1 earrings • Cut a 2½-in. (6.4 cm) piece of 22-gauge wire. Make a plain loop (Basics, p. 12) on one end. String a heart bead and make a wrapped loop (Basics, p. 12) that is perpendicular to the first loop.

2 Open a 4 mm jump ring (Basics, p. 12). Attach a heart charm and a soldered jump ring. Close the loop. Use another 4 mm jump ring to attach a second heart charm.

3 Open the bottom loop of the heart unit (Basics, p. 12). Attach the soldered jump ring and close the loop.

4 Open the loop of an earring wire. Attach the dangle and close the loop. Make a second earring.

Supplies

bracelet
- ◆ **6** 12–15 mm glass heart beads
- ◆ **14** 8–15 mm heart charms
- ◆ **4** 6 mm round crystals
- ◆ **6** 4 mm bicone crystals
- ◆ **2** 3 mm flat spacers
- ◆ flexible beading wire, .012 or .014
- ◆ 18 in. (46 cm) 22-gauge half-hard wire
- ◆ **3** 1½-in. (3.8 cm) head pins
- ◆ **7** 6 mm soldered jump rings
- ◆ **14** 4 mm jump rings
- ◆ **2** crimp beads
- ◆ **2** crimp covers
- ◆ toggle clasp
- ◆ chainnose and roundnose pliers
- ◆ diagonal wire cutters
- ◆ crimping pliers (optional)

earrings
- ◆ **2** 12–15 mm glass heart beads
- ◆ **4** 8–15 mm heart charms
- ◆ 5 in. (13 cm) 22-gauge wire
- ◆ **2** 6 mm soldered jump rings
- ◆ **4** 4 mm jump rings
- ◆ pair of earring wires
- ◆ chainnose and roundnose pliers
- ◆ diagonal wire cutters

Design alternative

Play up fiery colors with crystals and lampworked beads in shades of dark red coral.

❝I wear my heart on my sleeve, so why not on my wrist?**❞** –Alyce

Weave a
bloom-and-

Try this sweetly sophisticated spin on a daisy chain

by Heidi Bowen

This bracelet made with copper tubes, Czech glass leaves, and teardrop beads, creates gorgeous flowers for your wrist. The materials can also be flexible; I used vintage crystals at the center of each flower, but contemporary ones can be just as beautiful.

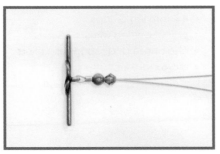

1 Cut a 48-in. (1.2 m) piece of beading wire. Center half of a clasp on the wire. Over both ends, string a crimp bead, a spacer, and a bicone crystal. Crimp the crimp bead (Basics, p. 12).

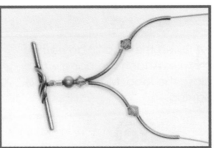

2 On each end, string a tube, a bicone, and a tube.

3 On one end, string a leaf bead. String the other end through the leaf in the opposite direction.

4 On one end, string two leaves. On the other end, string three leaves. String the first end through the last leaf in the opposite direction. Tighten the wire.

5 On one end, string two teardrop beads. String the other end through the teardrops in the opposite direction.

6 On one end, string two teardrops. On the other end, string four teardrops. String the first end through the last two teardrops in the opposite direction. Tighten the wire.

attice
bracelet

Supplies

- **16** 15 mm curved tube beads
- **18** 12 mm leaf beads, top drilled
- **24** 6 mm teardrop beads
- **3** 6 mm round or aspirin-shaped crystals
- **10** 4 mm bicone crystals
- **2** 4 mm large-hole round spacers
- flexible beading wire, .014 or .015
- **2** crimp beads
- magnetic or toggle clasp
- chainnose or crimping pliers
- diagonal wire cutters

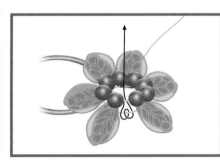

7 With each end, wrap around the wire between two leaves, exiting through the center of the flower.

8 On one end, string a round crystal. String the other end through the crystal in the opposite direction.

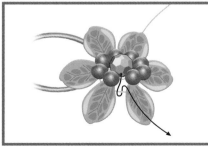

9 With each end, wrap around the wire between two leaves, exiting between the teardrop and leaf layers.

10 Repeat steps 2–9 twice. On each end, string a tube, a bicone, and a tube. Over both ends, string a bicone.

11 Over both ends, string a spacer, a crimp bead, and half of the clasp. Go back through the beads just strung and tighten the wire. Crimp the crimp bead and trim the excess wire.

Fall for the beauty of the GINKGO

At first glance, this necklace displays an unusual collection of colors. But the ginkgo leaf, symbolic of the unification of opposites, brings these differences together. It shimmers with shades of brown, purple, and turquoise to match the beads.

Fire-polished crystals in bold tones highlight a leaf pendant

by Suzann Sladcik Wilson

1 necklace • Cut a piece of beading wire (Basics, p. 12). Center a pendant on the wire.

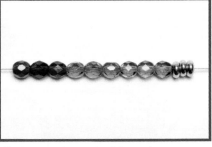

2 On each end, string nine crystals in three colors, then three spacers. Repeat until the strand is within 1 in. (2.5 cm) of the finished length.

3 On each end, string a crimp bead and half of a toggle clasp. Check the fit, and add or remove beads if necessary. Go back through the last few beads strung and tighten the wire. Crimp the crimp bead (Basics, p. 13) and trim the excess wire.

Supplies

necklace 17 in. (43 cm)
- 60–70 mm ginkgo leaf pendant
- **60–72** 6 mm fire-polished crystals, in three colors
- **18–24** 5–6 mm flat spacers
- flexible beading wire, .014 or .015
- **2** crimp beads
- toggle clasp
- chainnose or crimping pliers
- diagonal wire cutters

earrings
- **6** 6 mm round fire-polished crystals, **2** each in three colors
- **4** 5–6 mm flat spacers
- **2** 1½-in. (3.8 cm) head pins
- pair of lever-back earring wires
- chainnose and roundnose pliers
- diagonal wire cutters

1 earrings • On a head pin, string a spacer, three crystals in different colors, and a spacer. Make a plain loop (Basics, p. 12).

2 Open the loop of the dangle (Basics, p. 12). Attach the loop of an earring wire and close the loop. Make a second earring.

Design alternative

For another easy necklace option, string two or three leaves on 2–3 mm link chain. Include a fire-polished crystal with an AB finish to accent the iridescence in the leaves.

"Design for yourself and what you love. People always notice a piece that has been designed with passion and pride." —Suzann

215

STRING
dessert
first

Treat beads add sweet whimsy to a simple bracelet

by Cathy Jakicic

This bracelet is an ode to life's delicious pleasures. I started with red ceramic pillows mixed with golden beads that remind me of cinnamon toast. I used two-loop daisy spacers, sometimes called jangle spacers, to add pairs of whimsical treat beads. You can customize your bracelet to fit your own sweet tooth or string the whole dessert cart.

1 bracelet • Cut a piece of beading wire (Basics, p. 12). Center a jangle spacer, a disk bead, and a jangle spacer.

2a On each end, string a disk, a flat spacer, and a disk.
b Repeat the pattern from steps 1 and 2a until the strand is within 1 in. (2.5 cm) of the finished length.

3 On each end, add half of a clasp (Basics, p. 13).

Tips

• The ceramic disk beads are called "turtles" on the Clay River website (clayriverdesigns.com) and can be found under the "Etc." tab.
• Arrange the treat beads before you start attaching them to achieve a pleasing balance.

Supplies

bracelet
- ◆ **9–13** ½-in. (13 mm) ceramic disk beads
- ◆ **12–20** 10–16 mm treat beads
- ◆ **6–10** 12 mm 2-loop daisy (jangle) spacers
- ◆ **4–6** 3 mm flat spacers
- ◆ flexible beading wire, .014 or .015
- ◆ **12–20** 2-in. (5 cm) head pins
- ◆ **2** crimp beads
- ◆ toggle clasp
- ◆ chainnose and roundnose pliers
- ◆ diagonal wire cutters
- ◆ crimping pliers (optional)

red earrings
- ◆ **2** ½-in. (13 mm) ceramic disk beads
- ◆ **2** 12 mm jangle spacers
- ◆ **4** 3 mm flat spacers
- ◆ **2** 1½-in. (3.8 cm) head pins
- ◆ pair of earring wires
- ◆ chainnose and roundnose pliers
- ◆ diagonal wire cutters

treat earrings
- ◆ **2** ½-in. (13 mm) ceramic disk beads
- ◆ **2** 10–16 mm treat beads
- ◆ **2** 2-in. (5 cm) head pins
- ◆ pair of earring wires
- ◆ chainnose and roundnose pliers
- ◆ diagonal wire cutters

Treat beads from JP Imported, jpimported.com.

4 On a head pin, string a treat bead. Make the first half of a wrapped loop (Basics, p. 12). Make two treat-bead units per jangle spacer.

5 Attach a treat-bead unit to each jangle-spacer loop, completing the wraps as you go.

1 red earrings • On a head pin, string a flat spacer, a disk bead, and a flat spacer. Make a plain loop (Basics, p. 12).

2 Open the loop of the bead unit (Basics, p. 12) and attach one loop of a jangle spacer. Close the loop. Open the loop of an earring wire and attach the dangle. Close the loop. Make a second earring.

1 treat earrings • On a head pin, string a treat bead and a disk bead. Make a wrapped loop (Basics, p. 12).

2 Open the loop of an earring wire (Basics, p. 12). Attach the dangle and close the loop. Make a second earring.

Design alternative

Go straight to dessert by simply adding treat beads to a chain for a tasty charm bracelet.

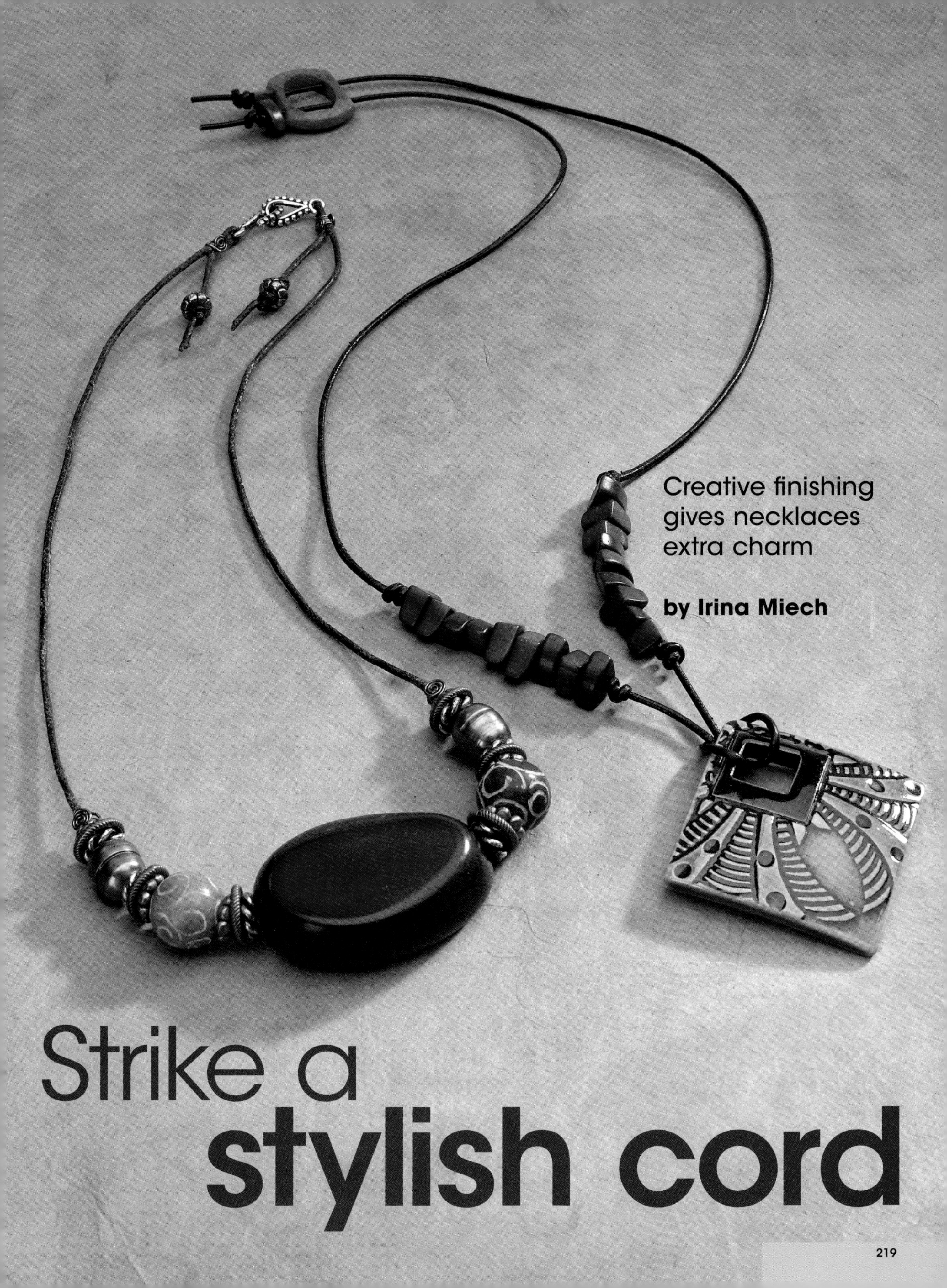

Creative finishing
gives necklaces
extra charm

by Irina Miech

Strike a
stylish cord

These necklaces are casually elegant and as easy to make as they are to wear. Start with some large-hole beads and components in warm, earthy colors, add some cord, and wrap things up with simple knotting or a flourish of wirework.

Supplies

ceramic-pendant necklace 24 in. (61 cm)

- 34 mm ceramic pendant
- 15 mm circle bead, double drilled
- **20** 8 mm tagua chips
- leather cord
- scissors

tagua nut necklace 20 in. (51 cm)

- 34 mm tagua nut bead
- **2** 8–10 mm carved round beads
- **2** 10 mm large-hole potato pearls
- **6** 9 mm decorative jump rings
- **4** 7 mm bead caps
- **6** 7 mm spacers
- **4** 6 mm spacers
- waxed linen cord
- 12 in. (30 cm) 24-gauge wire
- hook-and-eye clasp
- chainnose or flatnose pliers
- roundnose pliers
- diagonal wire cutters
- crayon or wax pencil
- scissors

Tip

Be sure to tie your knots as close to the beads as possible for a professional look.

1 ceramic necklace • Cut a 30–32-in. (76–81 cm) piece of cord. Fold the cord in half and string a pendant over the loop.

2 Bring the ends of the cord through the loop and tighten the cord.

3 On each side, about ¾ in. (1.9 cm) from the loop, tie one or two overhand knots (Basics, p. 12). String nine chips and tie one or two overhand knots.

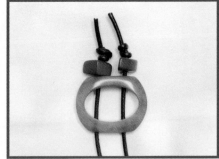

4 String each end through a double-drilled circle bead and string a chip. Check the fit and tie one or two overhand knots on each end. Trim the excess cord.

❝The visual weight of the cord balances the bold components beautifully. ❞ —Irina

1 tagua nut necklace • Cut a 20–22-in. (51-56 cm) piece of cord. Center a tagua nut bead. On each side, string: 7 mm spacer, 9 mm jump ring, 7 mm bead cap, carved bead, bead cap, jump ring, 7 mm spacer, pearl, 7 mm spacer, jump ring, 6 mm spacer.

2 With a crayon or wax pencil, mark the cord on each side next to the beaded section. Cut a 3-in. (7.6 cm) piece of wire. Center the wire over one of the marks, and wrap the ends around the cord three times.

3 Bend each end of the wire near the wraps to create a partial loop.

4 Use roundnose and chain-nose (or flatnose) pliers to make a small coil. Trim the excess wire. Repeat with the other end of the wire.

5 Flatten each coil against the wraps. Make another coiled wrap on the other side of the beads.

6 On each side, about 1½–2 in. (3.8–5 cm) from the end of the cord, string half of a clasp. Fold the cord and check the fit, adjusting the fold as needed. Secure with a coiled wrap as in steps 2–5. About ¾ in. (1.9 cm) from the coiled wrap, tie an overhand knot (Basics, p. 12). String a 6 mm spacer and tie an overhand knot. Trim the excess cord.

The softer side of
STEAMPUNK

A ceramic gear bead serves as both a focal piece and a clasp

by Lorelei Eurto

I love Elaine Ray's bronze and moss-colored beads. These five beauties make a subdued backdrop for Melanie Brooks' ceramic gear bead. With a little bit of wire, you can turn this funky focal bead into a clasp. The smaller gear beads work great for earrings and they spin like real gears.

1 bracelet • Cut a 3-in. (7.6 cm) piece of 18-gauge wire and fold it in half. On one end, string a round spacer. Over both ends, string a gear bead.

2 Bend each end of the wire against the back of the bead. On each end, grasp the wire with roundnose pliers just beyond the edge of the bead, and pull the wire around to make a loop.

3 Cut a piece of beading wire (Basics, p. 12). String a ceramic lentil bead, a flat spacer, a saucer bead, and a flat spacer. Repeat the pattern until the bracelet is within 2 in. (5 cm) of the finished length.

4 On one end, string two crimp beads and a hook clasp. Go back through the crimp beads and tighten the wire. Crimp the crimp beads (Basics, p. 13) and trim the excess wire.

5 Repeat step 4 on the other end, substituting the gear bead for the hook.

> **"Bead confidently. Don't second-guess your designs."**
> —Lorelei

1 earrings • Cut a 4-in. (10 cm) piece of wire. Center the wire on the third tier of a Right Angle mandrel or the barrel of a thick pen. Pull the ends around to form an elongated U.

2 On a bench block or anvil, hammer the curve of the wire. Turn the wire over and hammer the other side.

Supplies

bracelet

- 30 mm gear bead, center drilled, Earthenwood Studio, earthenwoodstudio.com.
- **5** 25 mm ceramic lentil beads
- **4–8** 8 mm saucer beads
- **8–16** 4 mm flat spacers
- 4 mm round spacer
- flexible beading wire, .018 or .019
- 3 in. (7.6 cm) 18-gauge wire
- **4** crimp beads
- hook clasp
- chainnose and roundnose pliers
- diagonal wire cutters
- crimping pliers (optional)

earrings

- **2** 19 mm gear beads, center drilled
- **2** 4 mm flat spacers
- **4** 3 mm round spacers
- 8 in. (20 cm) 20-gauge wire
- **2** crimp beads
- chainnose pliers
- diagonal wire cutters
- bench block or anvil
- file or emery board
- Fiskars Right Angle mandrel or thick pen
- hammer

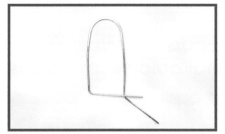

3 About 1 in. (2.5 cm) from one end, bend the wire to form a 90-degree angle. About 1 in. (2.5 cm) from the other end, bend the wire to form a 45-degree angle.

4 String: round spacer, flat spacer, gear bead, round spacer, crimp bead. Flatten the crimp bead (Basics, p. 13).

5 Make a 90-degree bend next to the crimp. About ¼ in. (6 mm) from each end, trim the wire. File the ends.

Tip

Rather than making one earring at a time, try working with two 4-in. (10 cm) wires together. You'll get more consistent results that way.

Design alternative

For a different take on a toggle clasp, use a time-wheel charm (earthenwoodstudio.com) and a game spinner (timholtz.com). By attaching a chain to the spinner, you can add length to your bracelet.

Highlight a
Valentine
bouquet

A bright floral pendant calls for unconventional colors

by Kristal Wick

Chartreuse is an unlikely color for a valentine. But in this stoneware heart, it provides a verdant background for a field of bright flowers. I glued a few flat-back crystals to the heart then strung cubes, bicones, and fabric beads to match.

Jazz up the pendant even more with flat-back crystals in topaz.

1 necklace • Open a jump ring (Basics, p. 12). Attach a heart pendant and close the jump ring. Cut a piece of beading wire (Basics, p. 13). Center two bicone crystals, the pendant, and two bicones.

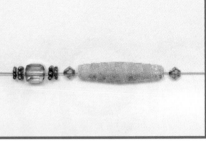

2 On each end, string: 3 mm spacer, 4 mm spacer, cube crystal, 4 mm spacer, 3 mm spacer, bicone, 25 mm fabric bead, bicone. Repeat until the strand is within 1 in. (2.5 cm) of the finished length, substituting a 13 mm fabric bead for the last 25 mm bead.

3 On each end, add half of a toggle clasp (Basics, p. 13).

1 earrings • On a head pin, string a bicone crystal, a 13 mm fabric bead, and a bicone. Make a plain loop (Basics, p. 12).

2 Trim the head from a head pin and make a plain loop. String: 3 mm spacer, 4 mm spacer, cube crystal, 4 mm spacer, 3 mm spacer, bicone. Make a plain loop perpendicular to the first loop.

3 Open the bottom loop of the cube unit (Basics, p. 12) and attach the fabric unit. Close the loop. Open the loop of the dangle and attach an earring wire. Close the loop. Make a second earring.

Supplies

necklace 19 in. (48 cm)
- 35 mm heart pendant
- **8** 25 mm Batik Beauties fabric beads
- **2** 13 mm Batik Beauties fabric beads
- **12–16** 6 mm cube crystals
- **26–30** 4 mm bicone crystals
- **24–32** 4 mm square spacers
- **24–32** 3 mm square spacers
- flexible beading wire, .014 or .015
- 10 mm jump ring
- **2** crimp beads
- toggle clasp
- **2** pairs of pliers
- diagonal wire cutters
- crimping pliers (optional)

earrings
- **2** 13 mm Batik Beauties fabric beads
- **2** 6 mm cube crystals
- **6** 4 mm bicone crystals
- **4** 4 mm square spacers
- **4** 3 mm square spacers
- **4** 1½-in. (3.8 cm) head pins
- pair of earring wires
- chainnose and roundnose pliers
- diagonal wire cutters

Swingy
chandeliers

Combine wirework and glass for stylish earrings

by Karen Galbraith

I love to experiment with different techniques to create unique jewelry. I was looking for a new way to make chandelier earrings when I hit upon the idea for the spirals. It's a great, clean style with that little something extra.

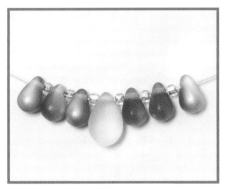

1 Cut a 3-in. (7.6 cm) piece of beading wire. Center a 9 mm teardrop. On each end, string an alternating pattern of three 11º seed beads and three 6 mm teardrops.

2 Cut a 4-in. (10 cm) piece of 22-gauge wire. Grasp the center of the wire with roundnose pliers and cross the ends of the wire to make a loop.

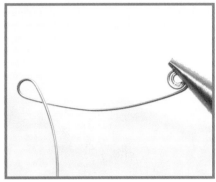

3 On one end of the wire, use the tip of your roundnose pliers to make a tiny loop. Use chainnose pliers to make a coil. Repeat on the other end.

4 On each end of the beaded strand, string a crimp bead and the center of a coil. Go back through the last few beads strung and tighten the wire. Crimp the crimp bead (Basics, p. 12) and trim the excess wire.

5 Use crimping pliers to gently close a crimp cover over each crimp.

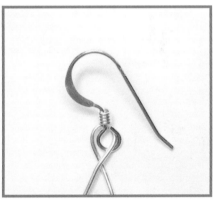

6 Open the loop of an earring wire (Basics, p. 12). Attach the dangle and close the loop. Make a second earring.

Supplies

- **2** 9 mm glass teardrops
- **12** 6 mm glass teardrops
- **12** 11º seed beads
- flexible beading wire, .014 or .015
- 8 in. (20 cm) 22-gauge wire
- **4** crimp beads
- **4** crimp covers
- pair of earring wires
- chainnose and roundnose pliers
- crimping pliers
- diagonal wire cutters

Tip

You can substitute fringe beads for the 6 mm teardrops.

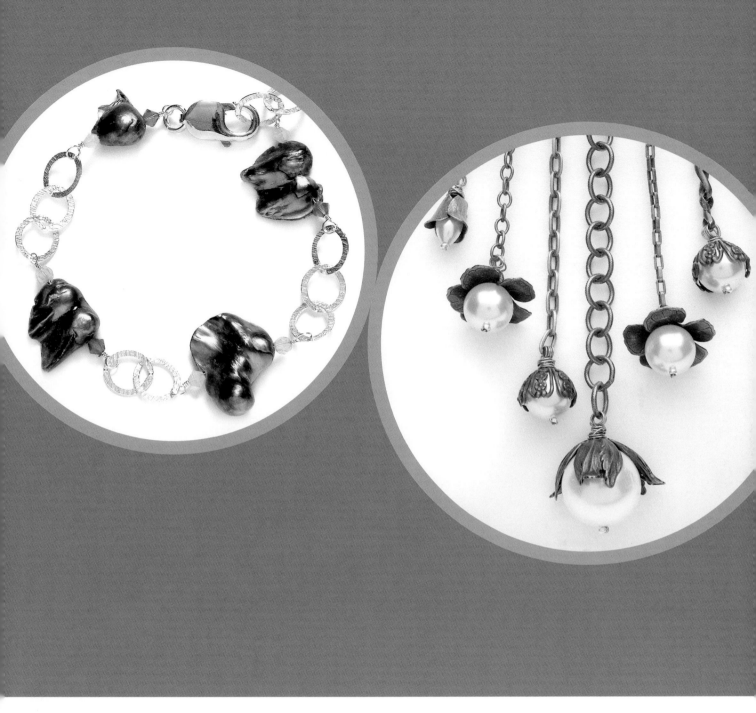

Pearls

"Black dyed jade and blackstone are also great options for opaque black beads."
—Miriam

Accessories in black and white or red and white match a wide variety of outfits.

RETRO
repurposed

What was old becomes new when you tie in mod materials

by Miriam Fuld

When I inherited a vintage onyx necklace, I envisioned this chic retrofit. I wanted the onyx to really stand out, and contrasting white glass pearls did the trick — plus, black and white is a classic combination. If you don't have any hand-me-down beads, glass or crystal pearls substitute nicely for onyx and offer you more color choices. Finish with ribbon for a trendy closure that allows you to wear your necklace at different lengths!

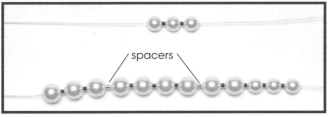

1 necklace • Cut a 24-in. (61 cm) piece of beading wire. String: 14 mm bead or pearl, spacer, 10 mm pearl, spacer, four 14 mms alternated with three spacers. Center the beads.

2 On each end, string: spacer, 10 mm, spacer, five 10 mms alternated with four 11º seed beads, spacer, 10 mm, 11º, 10 mm, 11º.

spacers

3 On one end, string three 8 mm pearls alternated with two 11ºs. On the other end, string: three 10 mms alternated with two 11ºs, spacer, four 10 mms alternated with three 11ºs, spacer, 10 mm, 11º, 10 mm, 11º, three 8 mms alternated with two 11ºs.

4 On each end, string a crimp bead and a decorative soldered jump ring. Check the fit, and add or remove beads if necessary. Go back through the last few beads strung and tighten the wire. Crimp the crimp bead (Basics, p. 12) and trim the excess wire. Close a crimp cover over each crimp if desired.

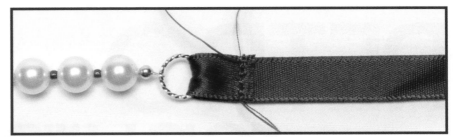

5 Cut a 17–19-in. (43–48 cm) piece of ribbon. Apply Dritz Fray Check, clear adhesive, or clear nail polish to the ends to prevent fraying. Let dry.

6a On one end, string a soldered jump ring from step 4. Using a sewing machine or needle and thread, sew the end of the ribbon to the back.

b Repeat steps 5 and 6a on the other end. To wear the necklace, tie the ribbons in a bow.

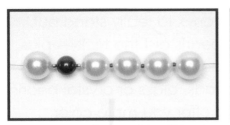

1 bracelet • Cut an 8-in. (20 cm) piece of beading wire. String: 14 mm bead or pearl, spacer, 10 mm pearl, spacer, four 14 mms alternated with three 11º seed beads.

2 On one end, string a crimp bead and a lobster claw clasp. Go back through the last few beads strung and tighten the wire. Crimp the crimp bead (Basics, p. 13) and trim the excess wire. Repeat on the other end, substituting a decorative soldered jump ring for the clasp. Close a crimp cover over each crimp if desired.

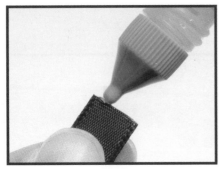

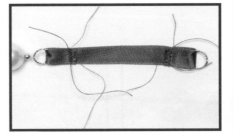

3 Cut a 4–5-in. (10–13 cm) piece of ribbon. Apply Dritz Fray Check, clear adhesive, or clear nail polish to the ends to prevent fraying. Let dry.

4 On one end of the ribbon, string the soldered jump ring from step 2. Using a sewing machine or needle and thread, sew the end of the ribbon to the back. On the other end, string a soldered jump ring. Check the fit, and trim ribbon if necessary. Sew the end of the ribbon to the back.

Design alternative

Crystal-accent rondelles are all the rage in pearl necklaces and they work beautifully in this design. Here I centered the large pearls for an intriguing balance of symmetry and asymmetry.

Tip

Don't care for needle and thread? Use crimp ends to attach the ribbon in the necklace and bracelet. Or string an extra-long ribbon through both rings, then tie a bow behind your neck.

1 earrings • On a head pin, string: 10 mm pearl, 8 mm pearl, spacer, 8 mm, spacer. Make a plain loop (Basics, p. 12).

2 Slide the loop of the dangle onto a kidney-style earring wire. Use chainnose pliers to pinch the loop of the earring wire closed. Make a second earring.

Supplies

necklace 18–19 in. (46–48 cm)
- ◆ **5** 14 mm round gemstone beads or glass or crystal pearls
- ◆ **26** 10 mm glass or crystal pearls
- ◆ **6** 8 mm glass or crystal pearls
- ◆ **1** g 11º seed beads
- ◆ **13** 2 mm round spacers
- ◆ flexible beading wire, .014 or .015
- ◆ ribbon, ³⁄₈ in. (1 cm) wide
- ◆ **2** 10–12 mm decorative soldered jump rings
- ◆ **2** crimp beads
- ◆ **2** crimp covers (optional)
- ◆ chainnose or crimping pliers
- ◆ diagonal wire cutters
- ◆ Dritz Fray Check, clear adhesive, or clear nail polish
- ◆ scissors
- ◆ sewing machine or needle and thread

bracelet
- ◆ **5** 14 mm glass or crystal pearls
- ◆ **10** mm glass or crystal pearl
- ◆ **3** 11º seed beads
- ◆ **2** 2 mm round spacers
- ◆ flexible beading wire, .014 or .015
- ◆ ribbon, ³⁄₈ in. (1 cm) wide
- ◆ **2** 10–12 mm decorative soldered jump rings
- ◆ **2** crimp beads
- ◆ **2** crimp covers (optional)
- ◆ lobster claw clasp
- ◆ chainnose or crimping pliers
- ◆ diagonal wire cutters
- ◆ Dritz Fray Check, clear adhesive, or clear nail polish
- ◆ scissors
- ◆ sewing machine or needle and thread

earrings
- ◆ **2** 10 mm glass or crystal pearls
- ◆ **4** 8 mm glass or crystal pearls
- ◆ **4** 2 mm round spacers
- ◆ **2** 1½-in. (3.8 cm) head pins
- ◆ pair of kidney-style earring wires
- ◆ chainnose and roundnose pliers
- ◆ diagonal wire cutters

Pearls rule

At first this necklace was going to be super long and asymmetrical with a focal bead on one side. The pearls had other ideas, and my necklace ended up much shorter with the focal bead at the center. I love when my materials lead me to make something completely different (and better) than the design I first envisioned.

Find design inspiration by obeying the beads

by Mia Gofar

3 On each end, string a crimp bead and the corresponding loop of half of a slide clasp. Check the fit, and add or remove beads if necessary. Go back through the last few beads strung and tighten the wire. Crimp the crimp bead (Basics, p. 12) and trim the excess wire.

1 necklace • Cut a 24-in. (61 cm) piece of beading wire for the shortest (top) strand. Cut three more pieces, each 2 in. (5 cm) longer than the last. On each wire, string a bicone crystal, a hole of a spacer bar, and a bicone. Center the beads.

2 On each end, string a pattern of twist pearls and bicones until the strand is within ½ in. (1.3 cm) of the finished length.

1 earrings • On a decorative head pin, string a crystal and a spacer. Make the first half of a wrapped loop (Basics, p. 12).

2 Cut a 2½-in. (6.4 cm) piece of wire. Make a wrapped loop. String a crystal and make a wrapped loop.

3 Cut a 2½-in. (6.4 cm) piece of wire. Make the first half of a wrapped loop. String a crystal and a spacer and make the first half of a wrapped loop.

4 Attach the bead units as shown and complete the wraps.

5 Open the loop of an earring wire (Basics, p. 12). Attach the dangle and close the loop. Make a second earring.

Supplies

necklace 18-22 in. (46-56 cm)
- 25–30 mm four-strand decorative spacer bar
- **180-200** 9 mm crystal twist pearls
- **60-80** 4 mm bicone crystals
- flexible beading wire, .014 or .015
- **8** crimp beads

- four-strand slide clasp
- chainnose or crimping pliers
- diagonal wire cutters

earrings
- **6** 8 mm crystals
- **4** 4 mm flat spacers
- 10 in. (25 cm) 24-gauge wire

- **2** 1½-in. (3.8 cm) decorative head pins
- pair of earring wires
- chainnose and roundnose pliers
- diagonal wire cutters

Design alternatives

The beads in your earrings don't have to match the beads in your necklace. Aim for a match in shape or color instead.

Keshi pearl
dangles

Embrace the beauty of imperfection

by Michelle Buettner

Pearls are amazing. Their beauty transcends time and trends, and their soft glow allows the wearer to sparkle. As I made my loops to attach the pearls to the chain, I did a sort of chaotic wrap that wasn't neat and orderly, but imperfect to match the organic pearls.

Tip
To make organic wraps, use your fingers instead of pliers to loosely wrap the wire.

1 For each earring: Cut a 5-in. (13 cm) piece of 24-gauge wire. String a pearl and bend the wires upward. With one end, make the first half of a wrapped loop (Basics, p. 12).

2 With the other end, make a set of loose wraps (Tip, previous page). Make five pearl units.

3 Cut a 1¼-in. (3.2 cm) piece of chain. Attach the loop of a pearl unit and an end link of chain. Complete the wraps.

4 Skip two links and attach a pearl unit. Attach the remaining pearl units, skipping a link between each. Complete the wraps as you go.

5 To make an earring wire: Cut a 2-in. (5 cm) piece of 20-gauge wire. Using the tip of your roundnose pliers, make a loop.

6 Place your roundnose pliers next to the loop and pull the wire around the pliers.

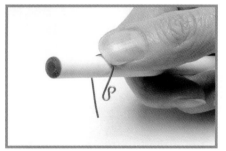

7 Place the barrel of a pen next to the loop from step 5 and pull the wire around the barrel. Use the tip of your chainnose or roundnose pliers to make a slight bend. Trim the excess wire and file the end.

8 On a bench block or anvil, hammer each side of the earring wire. File the end of the wire if necessary.

9 Open the loop of the earring wire (Basics, p. 12) and attach the dangle. Close the loop.

Supplies

- **10** 10–20 mm keshi pearls, center drilled
- 4 in. (10 cm) 20-gauge wire
- 50 in. (1.3 m) 24-gauge wire
- 3 in (7.6 cm) chain, 3–4 mm links

- chainnose and roundnose pliers
- diagonal wire cutters
- hammer
- bench block or anvil
- metal file or emery board
- pen

Go for baroque

Mix metals and irregularly shaped pearls in an elegant statement necklace

by Naomi Fujimoto

Experiment with a variety of bead sizes and textures.

I jumped at the chance to string together my favorite strands of irregularly shaped mauve pearls. I went for a contemporary bib punctuated with assorted brass and copper beads. Mix a rose gold clasp, antiqued-brass chain, gold-filled crimp beads — whatever you string, the combination of not-quite-matching shapes and colors will make your necklace look fresh.

1 necklace • Cut seven 12–14-in. (30–36 cm) pieces of beading wire (Basics, p. 12). On each wire, string 9–11 in. (23–28 cm) of pearls interspersed with bicone crystals and one or two metal beads. Stagger the placement of the metal beads within each strand.

2 Cut a 4-in. (10 cm) piece of 20-gauge wire. Make a wrapped loop (Basics, p. 12). Repeat.

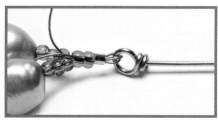

3 On one side, on each of two wires, string two or three 8º seed beads. Over both wires, string two 8ºs, a crimp bead, and a wrapped loop. Go back through the crimp bead and the two 8ºs and tighten the wires. Crimp the crimp bead (Basics, p. 12) and trim the excess wire.

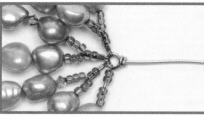

4 Repeat step 3 with the remaining pairs of wires on both sides of the necklace. Finish the seventh strand by itself.

Supplies

necklace 17½ in. (44.5 cm)
- ◆ **8–12** 20–40 mm metal beads
- ◆ **4–5** 16-in. (41 cm) strands 10–12 mm pearls
- ◆ **50–70** 4 mm bicone crystals
- ◆ **4** 4 mm rondelles
- ◆ **2 g** 8º seed beads
- ◆ bead cap
- ◆ flexible beading wire, .014 or .015
- ◆ 8 in. (20 cm) 20-gauge wire
- ◆ 1½-in. (3.8 cm) head pin
- ◆ **2** cones
- ◆ **12** crimp beads
- ◆ **4** Wire Guardians
- ◆ lobster claw clasp
- ◆ 3 in. (7.6 cm) chain, 12–15 mm links
- ◆ chainnose and roundnose pliers
- ◆ diagonal wire cutters
- ◆ crimping pliers (optional)

bracelet
- ◆ 20–25 mm metal bead
- ◆ **11–15** 10–12 mm pearls
- ◆ **9–13** 4 mm bicone crystals
- ◆ 15–17 mm hammered ring
- ◆ flexible beading wire, .014 or .015
- ◆ 2-in. (5 cm) head pin
- ◆ **2** crimp beads
- ◆ lobster claw clasp
- ◆ chainnose and roundnose pliers
- ◆ diagonal wire cutters
- ◆ crimping pliers (optional)

earrings
- ◆ **2** 10–12 mm pearls
- ◆ **2** 4 mm bicone crystals
- ◆ **2** bead caps
- ◆ **2** 1½-in. (3.8 cm) head pins
- ◆ pair of earring wires
- ◆ chainnose and roundnose pliers
- ◆ diagonal wire cutters

Supply notes

- For subtle sparkle, choose crystals that pick up the tones in the metal beads (not the pearls). I used bicones in jonquil satin and light peach satin to go with the brass and copper shades.
- I used beading wire in bronze.

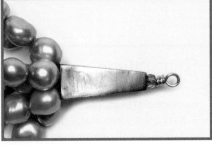

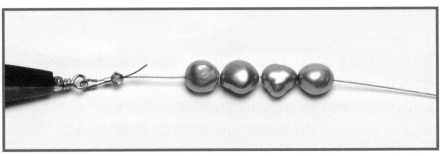

5 On each side, string a rondelle, a cone, and a rondelle. Make a wrapped loop.

6 Cut an 8–10-in. (20–25 cm) piece of beading wire. On one end, string a bicone, a crimp bead, a Wire Guardian, and one of the wrapped loops. Go back through the beads just strung, tighten the wire, and crimp the crimp bead. String pearls until the strand is within 1 in. (2.5 cm) of the finished length. Repeat on the other side.

7 Check the fit, and add or remove beads if necessary. On one end, string a bicone, a crimp bead, a Wire Guardian, and a lobster claw clasp. Repeat on the other end, substituting a 3-in. (7.6 cm) chain for the clasp. Go back through the beads just strung, tighten the wire, and crimp the crimp beads. Trim the excess wire.

8 On a head pin, string a pearl, a bead cap, and a bicone. Make the first half of a wrapped loop. Attach the dangle to the end link of chain and complete the wraps.

1 bracelet • Cut a piece of beading wire (Basics, p. 12). String pearls interspersed with bicone crystals until the strand is within 1½ in. (3.8 cm) of the finished length.

2 On one end, string a bicone, a crimp bead, a bicone, and a lobster claw clasp. Repeat on the other end, substituting a hammered ring for the clasp. Check the fit, and add or remove beads if necessary. Go back through the beads just strung and tighten the wire. Crimp the crimp beads (Basics, p. 13) and trim the excess wire.

3 On a head pin, string a metal bead and a bicone. Make the first half of a wrapped loop (Basics). Attach the hammered ring and complete the wraps.

1 earrings • On a head pin, string a pearl, a bead cap, and a bicone crystal. Make a wrapped loop (Basics, p. 12).

2 Open the loop of an earring wire (Basics, p. 12). Attach the dangle and close the loop. Make a second earring.

Try a simple bracelet (and earrings) to avoid pearl overkill.

"A medley of metal and pearls can liven up your winter wardrobe."
—Naomi

Design alternative

For dramatic earrings, fold a large filigree in half and attach a pearl unit where the ends meet. Use an 8–10 mm jump ring to attach the dangle.

It's all in the

Combine beads for maximum effect in this lush necklace

by Cathy Jakicic

Basic techniques can yield anything-but-basic results if you use the right materials and arrange them so they bring out the best in each other. The "work" in this necklace comes before you string the beads. Start with stick pearls and add glass teardrops with an iridescent finish. Continue the theme with opalescent bicone crystals. A gold pendant and a crystal focal piece tie it all together.

The AB finish of the teardrops brings out the luminescence of the pearls.

The tones of the brass pendant, spacers, and gold-plated findings unify the design.

66 The irregular shapes in a strand of stick pearls add excitement to simple stringing. **99** —Cathy

1

Cut a piece of beading wire (Basics, p. 12). On the wire, center one or two 4 mm spacers. On each end, string beads until the strand is within 2 in. (5 cm) of the finished length. String a second strand.

Color note
The crystal pendant is crystal golden shadow. The bicones are light grey opal AB.

mix

③

③ On each end of each wire, string a 4 mm spacer. On one side, over both wires, string a crimp bead and a lobster claw clasp. Go back through the last few beads strung and tighten the wires. Crimp the crimp bead (Basics, p. 13) and trim the excess wire. Repeat on the other end, substituting a soldered jump ring for the clasp.

Because most of the beads don't lie flush against each other, you'll have to do some adjusting before you tighten the wires at the end.

Use spacers sparingly. Too many will overpower the subtler colors of the beads.

The color of the Czech glass is similar to the crystal pendant.

A random arrangement of beads will be more interesting than a pattern, but make sure the quantities of each bead are roughly equal on both sides.

② Open a 10 mm jump ring (Basics, p. 12) and attach a leaf and a crystal pendant. Attach the center of both strands. Close the jump ring.

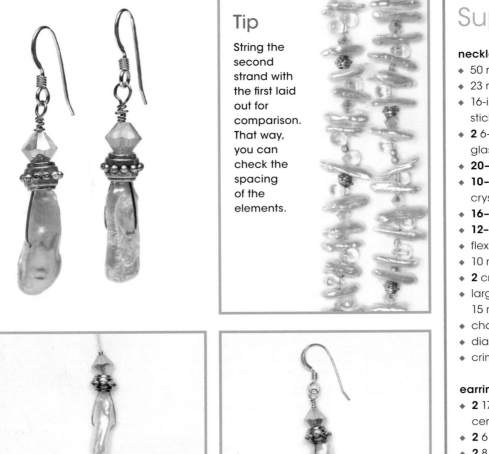

Tip

String the second strand with the first laid out for comparison. That way, you can check the spacing of the elements.

Supplies

necklace 18 in. (43 cm)

- 50 mm brass leaf pendant
- 23 mm crystal rock pendant
- 16-in. (41 cm) strand 17–21 mm stick pearls, center drilled
- **2** 6-in. (15 cm) strands 9 mm glass teardrop beads, AB finish
- **20–24** 6 mm bicone crystals
- **10–14** 4 mm Czech fire-polished crystals
- **16–20** 8 mm rondelle spacers
- **12–16** 4 mm round spacers
- flexible beading wire, .014 or .015
- 10 mm jump ring
- **2** crimp beads
- large lobster claw clasp and 15 mm soldered jump ring
- chainnose and roundnose pliers
- diagonal wire cutters
- crimping pliers (optional)

earrings

- **2** 17–21 mm stick pearls, center drilled
- **2** 6 mm bicone crystals
- **2** 8 mm rondelle spacers
- 8 in. (20 cm) 22-gauge half-hard wire
- pair of earring wires
- chainnose and roundnose pliers
- diagonal wire cutters

1 earrings • Cut a 4-in. (10 cm) piece of wire. On the wire, center a stick pearl. Bend the ends of the wire up. Over both ends, string a spacer and a bicone crystal. Wrap one end around the other twice. Trim the excess wire.

2 Make a wrapped loop (Basics, p. 12). Open the loop of an earring wire (Basics, p. 12). Attach the dangle and close the loop. Make a second earring.

Design alternative

You can get a fringed look by using top-drilled stick pearls. Or add some variety to the design by interspersing similarly shaped gemstones (these are labradorite) or, for subtle depth, try a few center-drilled stick pearls in a peach color.

Inexpensive pearls, scrap chain, and leftover crystals add up to a luxe look

by Cathy Jakicic

There are enough pearls on a 16-in. (41 cm) strand to skip the larger chain in back and string pearls all the way around.

Get a HOT LOOK at a COOL PRICE

A strand of these gorgeous blister pearls is less than $10. With bits of chain and a mix of crystals from another project, this necklace and earrings are a triumph of style over spending. Shopping note: Blister pearls are sometimes listed as baroque pearls.

Supplies

necklace 20 in. (51 cm)
- 16-in. (41 cm) strand 16–50 mm baroque pearls, top drilled
- **22–26** 3–8 mm crystals, in different shapes and colors
- flexible beading wire, .014 or .015
- 6–8-in. (15–25 cm) cable chain, 10 mm links
- 32–36 in. (81–91 cm) cable chain, 2 mm links
- 7 mm jump ring
- 1½-in. (3.8 cm) decorative head pin
- **2** crimp beads
- **2** Wire Guardians
- **2** crimp covers
- lobster claw clasp
- chainnose and roundnose pliers
- diagonal wire cutters
- crimping pliers (optional)

earrings
- 2 16–50 mm baroque pearls, top drilled
- **2** 4 mm bicone crystals
- **2** links cable chain, 10 mm links
- **2** 2-in. (5 cm) eye pins
- **2** 1½-in. (3.8 cm) decorative head pins
- pair of earring wires
- chainnose and roundnose pliers
- diagonal wire cutters

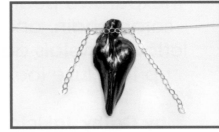

1 necklace • Cut a 3–4-in. (7.6–10 cm) piece of 2 mm-link chain. Cut a 17-in. (43 cm) piece of beading wire. On the wire, center a link about 1 in. (2.5 cm) from the end of the chain, a pearl, and a chain link about 1 in. (2.5 cm) from the first link.

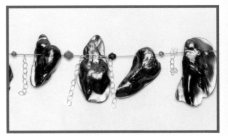

2 On each end, string about 13 in. (33 cm) of crystals, chains, and pearls, interspersing looped chains as in step 1. Cut the chains as you go so they are about the same length as the adjacent pearls.

3 Cut a 2–3-in. (5–7.6 cm) piece and a 4–5-in. (10–13 cm) piece of 10 mm-link chain. On each end of the beaded strand, string an 8 mm crystal, a crimp bead, and a piece of chain. Go back through the beads just strung and tighten the wire. Crimp the crimp bead (Basics, p. 12) and trim the excess wire.

4 Open a jump ring (Basics, p. 12) and attach the shorter chain and a clasp. Close the jump ring.

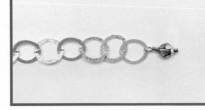

5 On a decorative head pin, string a crystal and make the first half of a wrapped loop (Basics, p. 12). Attach the remaining chain and complete the wraps.

6 Close a crimp cover over each crimp.

1 earrings • On an eye pin, string a pearl. Make the first half of a wrapped loop (Basics, p. 12).

2 Attach a chain link and complete the wraps.

3 On a decorative head pin, string a 4 mm bicone crystal. Make a plain loop (Basics, p. 12).

4 Open the loop of the bicone unit (Basics, p. 12) and attach the plain loop of the pearl unit. Close the loop. Attach the remaining loop to a chain link and complete the wraps.

5 Open the loop of an earring wire (Basics, p. 12). Attach the dangle and close the loop. Make a second earring.

❝I love how a blue spruce pearl reflects a range of blues and purples.❞ —Cathy

Design alternative

Silver peacock pearls and muted crystal colors let the silver chain play a more prominent role.

Tips

• It helps to remove irregularly shaped pearls from the strand and arrange a more pleasing pattern on your work surface. Cut the chain strands and place them between the pearls. Then add the bicone crystals, arranging the different sizes and colors to create a balanced look overall.

• Toward the center of the necklace, I strung a chain on each side of the crystals to give a little extra visual weight. After that, I strung a chain on one side only.

Colossal
pearls

Get two timely designs from the same strand of majestic beads

by Jane Konkel

Whether you choose to make a wide bib-style necklace, a long valance-style version, or both, you'll be layered in links and looking lovely in little time. These ginormous faux pearls come on a jumbo strand, so you can make both pieces for yourself and still have plenty of pearls left to make a glamorous gift.

1 horizontal necklace • On a head pin, string a spacer, a bead cap, a pearl or bead, and a bead cap. With the largest part of your roundnose pliers, make a plain loop (Basics, p. 12). Make 15–20 bead units.

2 Cut a 9-in. (23 cm) piece of oval-link chain for the shortest strand of your necklace. Cut four more pieces, each ½ in. (1.3 cm) longer than the previous piece.

3 Center the chains on your work surface and arrange the placement of the bead units before attaching them. Open the loop (Basics, p. 12) of a bead unit and attach the center link of the longest chain. Close the loop. Attach one to five bead units to each chain.

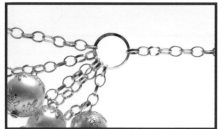

4 Open an end link of the longest chain and attach a circle link. Close the link. Attach one end of each remaining chain to the link. Attach the other end of each chain to another circle link.

Cut two 3–5-in. (7.6–13 cm) pieces of oval-link chain. Attach one to each circle link.

5 Check the fit, and trim chain if necessary. Remove a jump ring (Basics, p. 12) from the leftover circle-link chain and use it to attach half of a toggle clasp and an end link of chain. Close the jump ring. Repeat on the other end.

Tip

Use a neck form to help you arrange the placement of the bead units. It will also help you check the fit.

"Winter white and bright gold is a perfect pairing for the season."
—Jane

1 **vertical necklace** • Separate a five-link segment of circle-link chain by opening a jump ring (Basics, p. 12) in the chain. Repeat to remove a four-link segment, two three-link segments, and two two-link segments.

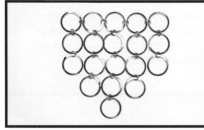

2 Attach the jump ring of the four-link segment to the center link of the five-link segment. Close the jump ring. On each side, attach a three-link segment and a two-link segment to the circle links.

3 Cut two 6–8-in. (15–20 cm) pieces of oval-link chain. Open an end link of each chain and attach a circle link as shown. Close the link.

4 Make five bead units as in step 1 of the horizontal necklace. Open the loop of a bead unit (Basics, p. 12) and attach a bottom circle link. Close the loop. Attach the remaining bead units to the circle links.

Attach half of a toggle clasp to each end as in step 5 of the horizontal necklace.

Design alternative

I used a variety of chain, pearl, and bead cap styles in this brass version of my vertical necklace.

Tip

The brass bead caps are meant to fit 15–18 mm beads; they were too small to fit these 22 mm pearls. Enlarging them by sliding them onto the pearls scratched the surface of the pearls. Instead, enlarge the bead caps by gently pressing each into a dapping block with a dapping punch.

"Let your necklace make the statement, and go easy on the earrings." —Jane

Supplies

horizontal necklace 16 in. (41 cm)

- **15–20** 22 mm faux pearls or round beads
- **15–20** 4 mm flat spacers
- **30–40** 17 mm leaf-style bead caps
- **2** 20 mm circle links and **2** jump rings, removed from circle-link chain
- **56–60** in. (1.4–1.5 m) oval-link chain, 7 mm links
- **15–20** 2-in. (5 cm) head pins
- toggle clasp
- chainnose and roundnose pliers
- diagonal wire cutters

vertical necklace 16 in. (41 cm)

- **5** 22 mm faux pearls or round beads
- **5** 4 mm flat spacers
- **10** 17 mm leaf-style bead caps
- 16 in. (41 cm) circle-link chain, 20 mm links
- 12–16 in. (30–41 cm) oval-link chain, 7 mm links
- **5** 2-in. (5 cm) head pins
- toggle clasp
- chainnose and roundnose pliers
- diagonal wire cutters

Contributors

Lori Anderson is a full-time jewelry designer living in Easton, Md. She is the creator of the Bead Soup Blog Party and author of the accompanying book. Visit her at www.PrettyThingsBlog.com or www.LoriAnderson.net.

As a world traveler, **Rupa Balachandar** likes to create jewelry that makes a statement. She regularly travels through Asia looking for components.

Angela Bannatyne is a jewelry designer and owns Gemstone & Bead Imports in Orlando, Fla., where she lives with her husband, two daughters, and dog. Contact her at renegadegirl1@aol.com or visit avenueacollection.com or avenuea.etsy.com.

Heidi Bowen's venture into the world of beads began young. At 17, Heidi opened Garden of Beadin' in Butte, Montana. After studying business and fashion merchandising, Garden of Beadin' opened in Bozeman and Missoula, Montana. You can find Heidi beadin' at her newest store in Bothell, Washington and contributing to beading publications. Contact her via owner@beadinseattle.com.

Suzanne Branca owns A Grain of Sand, a Web-based store that sells vintage and contemporary beads and findings. When she's not playing with beads, she loves to play with her grandbaby, Jaxon. Contact Suzanne at suzanne@agrainofsand.com or visit agrainofsand.com.

Wenche Brennbakk is a chemical engineer with passion for jewelry making. She lives in Norway and can be contacted at wdesign@live.no or via her website, www.WencheDesign.etsy.com.

Michelle Buettner is a jewelry artist with a Pearls Diploma from the Gemological Institute of America (GIA), who enjoys designing earring wires and findings as well as blogging about her creative process. Contact Michelle at Shel@asicj.com or visit MiShelDesigns.com.

Christianne Camera's biggest beading challenge is coming up with new designs. Her solution: buying supplies. Contact Christianne in care of Kalmbach Books.

The owner of SAC Motifs, **Sharon A. Clark** lives in Metamora, Mich., and teaches regularly at Glass with Class, Alada Beads, and Beadifferent Boutique. She also teaches at the Bead&Button Show. Contact Sharon at sac_motifs@yahoo.com or visit sacmotifs.com.

Elizabeth Del Monte lives with her husband and two sons in Coral Gables, Fla. She learned basic stringing to turn some of her mother's broken jewelry into new pieces. Contact Elizabeth at edelmonte@bellsouth.net or visit elizabethdelmonte.etsy.com.

Jill Erickson is a freelance writer, editor, and jewelry designer, Contact her via her website, jlerickson.com.

As a self-taught jewelry designer, **Lorelei Eurto** is always trying new techniques and tricks to make unique jewelry. Working full time in an art museum, Lorelei is never more than a foot away from inspiration. Read her daily blog at http://Lorelei1141.blogspot, or shop her etsy store at www.LoreleiEurtoJewelry.etsy.com.

Naomi Fujimoto is Senior Editor of *Bead Style* magazine and the author of Cool Jewels: Beading Projects for Teens. Visit her blog at cooljewelsnaomi.blogspot.com, or contact her in care of BeadStyle.

Miriam Fuld lives in Israel with her husband, four children, and their black Cocker-Pinscher. Contact Miriam at mim@mimzdesign.com or visit mimzdesign.com.

Kerri Furh is a full-time lampworked-bead artist and has been creating beads for more than 10 years. Contact Kerri at kerribeads@kerrifuhr.com or visit kerrifuhr.com.

In a household of full of boys, **Karen Galbraith** began creating jewelry as a way to express her girly side. Visit her website, www.JumpingJunebug.com.

Allyson Giesen is a working jewelry artist and owner of Beading Dreams, a retail bead store and design studio in Dallas, TX. Contact Allyson at beadingdreams@gmail.com or visit beadingdreams.com.

Mia Gofar lives in Singapore and is the author of several how-to jewelry books in Indonesia. Her first book was released in 2005, and she continues to write books today. Contact Mia via e-mail at mia@miagofar.com, or visit her website, miagofar.com or miamoredesign.com.

Linda Gunderman's career was in business. She started beading to get her mind off fibromyalgia pain, and it helped. Contact her at beadeddesignsbylinda@gmail.com or visit beadeddesignsbylinda.etsy.com.

Sherri Haab is a best-selling craft author with over 23 published books to her credit, with several selling over a million copies each. Visit her website, sherrihaab.com.

Beki Haley specializes in off-loom bead-weaving techniques but is happy to create in whichever way her muse takes her. Along with her husband, Shawn, and their children she owns and operates Out On A Whim, a bead and jewelry supply company. Contact info@whimbeads.com or visit www.whimbeads.com.

Monica Han is an award-winning mixed-media jewelry designer and teacher in Potomac, Md. She is also a CREATE YOUR STYLE with SWAROVSKI CRYSTAL ELEMENTS Ambassador. Contact her via e-mail at mhan@dreambeads.biz.

Leah Hanoud has been beading for more than 15 years and has a B.F.A. with a concentration in jewelry and metalsmithing from the University of Massachusetts. She has worked her entire beading career at Turquoise-StringBeads in Fall River, Mass. Contact Leah at (508) 677-1877 or turq2000@turquoise-stringbeads.com, or visit turquoise-stringbeads.com.

Melissa Hathcock's hobby became a business while she was in the bread aisle of her Houston, Texas, grocery store. While she was shopping, a woman commented on her necklace and purchased it on the spot! To view her work, visit melissahathcockdesigns.com.

Jamie Hogsett is a bead lover, jewelry designer, beading instructor, freelance editor, and the Education Coordinator for Soft Flex Company. She is the author of *Show Your Colors, Stringing Style*, and co-author, with Marlene Blessing, of books in the *Create* series. Contact her at jhogsett@yahoo.com.

Contact **Criss Hunt** at info@handmade-beads.com or visit handmadebeads.com.

Cathy Jakicic is Editor of *Bead Style* magazine and the author of the book Hip Handmade Memory Jewelry. She has been creating jewelry for more than 15 years. Contact her via e-mail at cjakicic@beadstyle.com.

Karen Karon studies many aspects of jewelry-making and silversmithing. She is a certified PMC artisan and chain mail artist, and she teaches classes in both techniques. Visit her website, karenkaron.com.

Susan Lenart Kazmer is an internationally-recognized mixed-media jewelry artist, silversmith, and teacher. She's developed many "cold-join" techniques over the years to transform found objects into works of art. Visit her website, slkartmechanic.com.

Jane Konkel is Associate Editor of *Bead Style*, and contributed several new designs to the book *Bead Journey*. Contact her via e-mail at jkonkel@beadstyle.com.

Aga Kruk moved to Arlington, Va., from Poland five years ago and has been designing jewelry ever since. She teaches jewelry classes in Virginia and has recently launched an online gallery. Contact her at aga@agajewelrydesigns.com or visit www.agajewelrydesigns.com.

Contact **Sonia Kumar** at soniakumar92@yahoo.com.

Kelsey Lawler is an assistant editor at *Bead Style* magazine. Contact her at klawler@kalmbach.com.

Jess Italia Lincoln is the educator for Vintaj. She teaches workshops in Galena, Ill. Contact Jess at design@vintaj.com or visit the Vintaj blog and idea gallery at vintaj.com for more inspiration.

Mary Lynn Maloney is a jewelry designer and mixed-media artist. Her CelticBelle jewelry line features authentic postage stamps and coins from Ireland, and can be found in the artist's Etsy shop. Contact Mary Lynn at mlm@topfloordesigns.net

An event planner in Phialdelphia, Pa., **Gretchen McHale** has come a long way from the days when she raided her dad's fishing box for supplies. Contact her at gretchen@studio320jewelry.com.

Lori Mendenhall creates artsy and eye-catching jewelry in her California studio. She loves to experiment with unique materials and designs. Visit www.lorimendenhall.com, or contact Lori via lorimendenhall@cox.net

Irina Miech is an artist, teacher, and the author of many books on jewelry making. She also oversees her retail bead supply business and classroom studio, Eclectica and The Bead Studio in Brookfield, Wis., where she teaches classes in beading, wirework, and metal clay. Contact Irina at Eclectica, 262-641-0910, or via e-mail at eclecticainfo@sbcglobal.net.

Nina Lara Novikova is an amature jewelry designer from Kirkland, Wash. She loves working with silver and gemstones because of the bold and colorful design possibilities. She can be contacted at nina_lara@msn.com, or visit her website, http://www.etsy.com/shop/ninalara.

Dee Perry has been in the bead business for 22 years. Seeing a need for unusual clasps, she started designing designer clasps and components seven years ago. Her unique designs can be purchased from Claspon-Claspoff.com, 954-880-0880.

Contact **Leah Rivers** at nina@ninadesigns.com, or visit her website, ninadesigns.com.

Brenda Schweder is the author of *Steel Wire Jewelry*, *Junk to Jewelry*, and *Vintage Redux*. She has been published over 100 times in books and magazines, and she also pens a column for *Wirework* magazine. Brenda teaches internationally and is a CREATE YOUR STYLE with SWAROVSKI Elements Ambassador. Visit her website, www.BrendaSchweder.com.

Alyce Shepardson belongs to the Santa Cruz Bead Society and enjoys gardening and cooking. Alyce also has a full-time job working for a custom home builder. Contact Alyce at alycesjewelrydesigns@gmail.com or visit designsbyalyce.com.

A former public school instructor, **Kim St. Jean** now combines her love of teaching with her talent as a jewelry maker. She teaches metalworking and other jewelry-making techniques across the U.S. and, when she's not traveling, at her studio in Myrtle Beach, SC. Kim is the author of *Mixed Metal Mania* and *Metal Magic*. Contact her at kim@kimstjean.com or through her website, kimstjean.com.

Debbie Tuttle is a full-time jewelry artist who creates her own vintage-inspired

jewelry in Charlton, N.Y. Contact her via e-mail at bijouxcreations@hotmail.com, or visit her website, bijouxcreationscom.

Jenny Van is a microbiologist and jewelry designer based in Huntington Beach, Calif. Contact her via e-mail at jenny@beadsjcom, or visit beadsj.com.

Suzanne Walters lives in Canon City, Colo. Her favorite jewelry-making materials are crystals and metal. Contact Suzanne via email at zannewalters@gmail.com or visit Suzanne's Design Studio at mimisgems.com.

Kimberly Wayne lives in New Berlin, Wis., with her two dogs, Mya and Layla. She works at Eclectica bead store in Brookfield, Wis., and also does freelance interior design. Contact Kimberly at theblonde@hotmail.com.

Donna Weeks is the co-owner with her daughter, Amy, of Old Sage Farm. They teach classes in beading, wirework, metalsmithing, mosaics, altered art, and watercolor. Contact her at donnaweeks1@yahoo.com or visit oldsagefarm.com.

Stacy Werkheiser is an associate editor at *Bead&Button* Magazine. Contact her at swerkheiser@kalmbach.com.

Ann Westby started making jewelry in 2001 and quickly discovered she had a passion for wire work. Contact her via her website, www.annwestby.com.

Diane Whiting is an award-winning original CREATE YOUR STYLE with SWAROVSKI Elements Ambassador, teacher, and contributor to numerous magazines. Contact her at dwhitingdesigns@cox.net or visit sparklesandsmiles.blogspot.com.

A Swarovski Ambassador, Internationally award-winning designer, author, and teacher, **Krystal Wick** has written books, DVDs, contributed to publications, and invented Sassy Silkies fabric beads. Contact her at kristal@kristalwick.com.

Joan Williams is a self-taught artist and jewelry designer living in the Missouri Ozarks. She can be reached at jww616@yahoo.com or lilruby.etsy.com.

Suzann Sladcik Wilson is the CEO and lead designer of Beadphoria. Contact her at suzann@beadphoria.com or visit beadphoria.com.

Index

Mixed